Hungering and Thirsting for Justice

You're blessed when you're at the end of your rope.
With less of you there is more of God and his rule.

You're blessed when you feel you've lost what is most dear to you.
Only then can you be embraced by the One most dear to you.

You're blessed when you're content with just who you are—no more, no less.
That's the moment you find yourselves proud owners
of everything that can't be bought.

You're blessed when you've worked up a good appetite for God.
He's food and drink in the best meal you'll ever eat.

You're blessed when you care.
At the moment of being "care-full," you find yourselves cared for.

You're blessed when you get your inside world—your mind and heart—put right.
Then you can see God in the outside world.

You're blessed when you can show people
how to cooperate instead of compete or fight.
That's when you discover who you really are,
and your place in God's family.

You're blessed when your commitment to God provokes persecution.
The persecution drives you even deeper into God's kingdom.

Matthew 5:2-10 (*The Message*)

Hungering and Thirsting for Justice

Real-Life Stories by Young Adult Catholics

Edited by
Lacey Louwagie & Kate Ward

Dedications

In loving memory of Sister Marian Louwagie, CSJ,
whose life inspired me to love fully and seek justice always.
—Lacey Louwagie

To my parents, who taught me how to write, edit, and create community,
and what it means to hunger and thirst for justice.
—Kate Ward

Hungering and Thirsting for Justice
Real-Life Stories by Young Adult Catholics
Edited by Lacey Louwagie and Kate Ward

Cover artwork and design by Tom A. Wright
Text design and typesetting by Patricia A. Lynch

Copyright © 2012 Lacey Louwagie and Kate Ward

Published by ACTA Publications, 4848 N. Clark Street, Chicago, IL 60640, (800) 397-2282, www.actapublications.com

Library of Congress Catalogue Number: 2012944506
ISBN: 978-0-87946-491-2
Printed in the United States of America by Versa Press
Year 25 24 23 22 21 20 19 18 17 16 15 14 13 12
Printing 20 19 18 17 16 15 14 13 12 11 10 9 8 7 6 5 4 3 2 First

Contents

Introduction

Fall of 2001 found both editors of this anthology in college—Kate in her first semester, and Lacey beginning her final year. The September 11 attacks on the World Trade Centers made it a difficult time for all Americans, but Catholics walked in a double darkness. Our Church was exploding around us with stories of sexual abuse by priests and, worse yet, systematic and long-lasting cover-ups of that abuse by our trusted leaders, the bishops. In Boston, the epicenter of all that was becoming known, Kate's friends asked her, "How can you stay?" But she remembered the first Sunday after September 11, when Catholic students packed the church as the campus priest helped everyone find a glimmer of hope, leading them in prayers for peace. Kate knew there was still so much good in the Church. But how could she make the case for the Church in the face of so much evil?

Many of us young adults who remained Catholic in those days felt a need to learn more about our faith—its history and its practice—in the midst of the growing crisis. Kate checked saints' biographies out of the library and taught herself how to pray the Rosary. She engaged in long, late-night prayer sessions, on which she would like to, but probably shouldn't, blame some of her dismal freshman grades. She also found vibrant campus ministers and thoughtful, committed Catholic students who encouraged her in her searching. From the other students, she learned the deep peace of Taizé prayer and the hokey glee of Pope jokes. As the Massachusetts bishops banned gay and lesbian couples from adopting through Catholic Charities and (unsuccessfully) fought against same-sex marriage in the state, Kate listened as some of her most devout Catholic friends shared their pain in loving a Church that opposed their dreams of falling in love and starting families. She found a community to pray with, to talk with, to share her questions.

Lacey grew up in a conservative parish that insisted Catholicism was about answers instead of questions. Still, as the congregation prayed for vocations and listened to laments about the priest shortage every week, her first big question emerged: Why does the priesthood leave so many people out? When she was ten years old, her parish priest gave an emphatic homily about why women couldn't become priests (because Jesus was a man) in response to her persistent questions. That answer didn't satisfy, and starting in college she "took to the pulpit" by giving speeches, doing research, and writing essays and letters about women's ordination. But she also clung to the reassurance of ancient Catholic traditions. In the days following September 11, Lacey turned to a habit that had comforted her since she was thirteen—falling asleep to the rhythm of the prayers of the Rosary as it slipped through her fingers, awaking to find the familiar indentations in her skin left from clutching the beads all night long.

The two of us still have so many questions. Why do some bishops deny communion to politicians who are pro-choice, but never to those who are pro-death penalty? Why do some Catholic employers, heirs to the social thought of Pope Leo XIII, union-bust and lay off workers as if their Catholic identity had nothing to do with their business practice? In a nation of great wealth and staggering economic inequality, why aren't more Catholics shouting our social gospel from the rooftops and why isn't (it sometimes seems) anybody hearing the few who are?

Thank God for beloved communities who accompany us on the search for justice. Kate has been blessed by being part of a wonderful prayer group in Chicago, while Lacey never stops being thankful for a late aunt who was a questioning nun and an uncle who is a listening priest.

We both belong to a national family of young people seeking Church reform, and we edit a group blog of young adults musing on the joys and sorrows of life as Catholics who hunger and thirst for justice. (Come visit us online at youngadultcatholics-blog.com.)

One day, a moving, funny piece by one of our blog's contributors, Justin Sengstock, caught the eye of Gregory Pierce, president of ACTA Publications in Chicago, a publisher of books for the Catholic/Christian market. He contacted us and suggested we put together this book, and now we joyfully offer you a sampling of ten original stories from this small community, in print for the first time: ten dialogue partners on the search for justice. We hope their stories will inspire you to learn more about the causes that move them, perhaps to become involved. More than that, we hope their stories will inspire you to find the place where God gives you the quiet determination of Katherine Schmidt, the mystical hope of Erin Lorenz, the joyful certainty of Phillip Clark. The world needs each of us to hunger and thirst for justice and, like these writers, to answer the call of that hunger.

Common themes emerged—some expected, some less so—as we read the submissions we'd collected. Having both gone through our own experiments with traditional piety, we smiled in recognition when we read of José Martinez's pocket Rosary and Justin Sengstock's prayers in Latin. Like the two of us did, both men learned that faith grows in surprising ways, no matter how you pray. The SOA/WHINSEC protest was a touchstone for a number of our writers (although the name has changed, the protest continues).

And anyone wondering whether Catholic education still presents a unique experience to young people should pick up this book and put their mind at rest. In fact, we joked that we should call it, "How Catholic College Made Me a Radical!" Catholic colleges were where Magalí Del Bueno found her calling as a witness for other immigrants and where Anna Zaros learned about peacebuilding, a passion that would take her halfway across the world. And not all of our writers took their experiences in the same direction. Lauren Ivory worked hard as a justice activist and only later discerned her true calling to chaplaincy, helping people one on one. Yet Bill Przylucki, who still thinks "almost daily" about the activists by his side in college, calls activism something he is "born to do." When he hears himself referred to as a "social-justice Catholic," he asks the question that unifies all of our stories: "Is there another kind of Catholic?"

Our writers strive to find their place within a Church and in a world that does not always hear the voices of those who cry for justice. Secure in her own stance against the death penalty, Katherine Schmidt struggled with the apathy of her fellow students, including future priests. Anna Zaros found that her American citizenship made her a suspect peacebuilder in the eyes of some Filipino colleagues. Johanna Hatch is aware that her activism as a clinic escort diminishes her in the eyes of many Catholics, yet she also hesitates to share her faith with her fellow volunteers, seeking out a place for herself on the margins.

Catholics in America, a recent study of American Catholics led by a professor at Catholic University of America, asked respondents whether they agreed with the statement, "I cannot imagine being anything but Catholic." Sixty-nine percent of the youngest generation of Catholics surveyed—folks born no earlier than 1979—agreed. This deep commitment to their Catholic identity shines through in our writers, despite their questions, disappointment, and sometimes downright holy anger with the institutional Church.

We see this fidelity in the ways Erin Lorenz remembers important events happening not in March of a certain year but during Lent, and Phillip Clark turns to the *Catechism of the Catholic Church* as a first resource when he questions his own identity. Johanna Hatch and Anna Zaros, inspired by the charisms of the women religious who taught them, discern their own vocations as laywomen. Magalí Del Bueno's encounters with immigrants bring to mind biblical images of the Holy Family's flight to Egypt, and José Martinez's prayerful words from the Mass apply to all activists: "We wait in joyful hope."

This book might seem to read like a roll call of painful growing issues within the Church: immigrant justice, women's ordination, abortion, acceptance of gay people, discouragement with Church hierarchy. Our call for submissions, however, didn't mention any of these issues. What you have in this book is simply what we got when we asked young Catholics what makes them hunger and thirst for justice. These are the issues we young Catholics are thinking about, praying over, and living through in our daily lives. Take these stories for what they are, in the spirit in which they were written.

The contributors to this volume are part of the Body of Christ: young and energetic, ready to love, ready to march, ready to sit and listen. They reflect the entire people of God: funny, thoughtful, sad, resigned, boiling over with anger, faithful and faith-filled.

Like it or not, this is who we young adult Catholics are and why we are still here: for the Church, for the justice for which we hunger and thirst, for and because of one another.

Lacey Louwagie and Kate Ward, Editors
July 14, 2012
Feast of St. Kateri Tekakwitha

Asking Questions and Taking Action

Bill Przylucki

When folks ask me why I became a community organizer, they are usually wondering why I'd work eighty-hour weeks in some of LA's poorest areas for relatively low pay. It's a straightforward question, but I used to fumble the answer. I thought people might as well have been asking me, "Why be alive?" I'm often tempted to answer, "Because God said so."

Two key experiences brought me to this point. Both came to me through God by way of the Church. In the first story, I saw the unending love God has for all of us, and the wonderful and creative ways our Church acts out that love even in the face of an incomprehensibly cruel world. The second story, from my time as an undergraduate, showed me how money and secular influence can endanger our Church's ability to be a vehicle of that love. I'm grateful that God arranged these experiences and put me on a path to take action for justice in the world and in the Church.

My childhood friend, Barbara, was just a little bit younger than me. We would play whenever our parents were at work together. My dad worked for Catholic Charities in Albany, New York, and Barbara's mom was a Sister of Mercy in the same diocese. I didn't think it was strange that Barbara's mom was a nun—I didn't know how remarkable her whole story was. Barbara's biological mother died of AIDS in 1988, leaving Barbara an orphan. A lot of fear and mystery still surrounded HIV and AIDS. Barbara's social workers were unable to find any "traditional" families willing to adopt her. So Sr. Mary Ann was given permission to become Barbara's mom.[1] The adoption was possible because the Sisters of Mercy and Bishop Howard Hubbard were incredibly progressive in thinking about how the diocese could be an instrument of God's love for this little girl.

Barbara's situation seemed logical to me. In Sunday school, I learned that when somebody is in need, the Church is supposed to help. I grew up across the street from my parish church, and my dad worked for the bishop. Right down the street were the nuns, my parish priest, and the bishop I looked up to as role models. They seemed part of my extended family, and I loved them. Why wouldn't they have helped Barbara?

In the last days of the summer of 1993, just a few weeks before I started third grade, my dad told me Barbara had died. A year earlier, he had explained that Barbara had a disease called AIDS and that this might happen. That's when I first started asking the big question: Why do people have to die of diseases?

I learned about AIDS annually in health class throughout the next decade, and every year the disease became less and less a death sentence and more and more a chronic condition. As the research and treatment options improved, I wondered why our society hadn't done these things sooner.

My dad was very involved with AIDS activism in the '80s and '90s. Every year, he took me to an AIDS quilt event to commemorate those who had died of the disease. A poster that hung in his office read, "The Body of Christ has AIDS." When he talked about the issue, he had a lot of hurt in his voice, the type of hurt that was holding down a burning anger.

Now that I know the history of the AIDS epidemic, I understand why

---

1   You can read more about Barbara's story in Sr. Mary Ann's book, *That Place Called Home: A Very Special Love Story*. Charis Books/Servant Publications, 2000.

my dad was angry. He was angry that we didn't act quickly enough. When rich people in Washington thought that this was a disease that only attacked gay people, and black people, and poor people, they debated what we should do about it. "How should we handle this?" they asked, as if the answer wasn't completely obvious. They even suggested trying to quarantine all AIDS patients in a segregated colony!

I am sure that with adequate support medical research could have made HIV and AIDS more manageable much earlier. Educating the general public could have spared thousands from discrimination and stigma. The government could have provided housing for many who died homeless, and they could have made it easier for Barbara to get adopted by a "normal" family. There never seemed to be much doubt that we would get there *eventually*, but that didn't help all those who suffered while our government and our society dragged our feet. We didn't take action in time for Barbara, and for thousands of others like her.

> I asked a lot of "why" questions to make sense of the malaise that I saw.... My family and the Church answered a lot of those questions.

As I grew up, I saw this inaction wasn't unique to the AIDS epidemic. It was a pattern. Our country's leaders asked stupid questions a lot—about global warming and terrorism and poverty and all kinds of things. Whenever I heard these questions being asked in Washington or Albany, Barbara's deeply buried memory would stir inside me and I'd feel that same sad anger that my dad felt when I was young.

I went to Albany's majority-black public schools. I got an education that was equal parts book smarts and street smarts. Mostly that meant being in a freer and more diverse community where I learned to play cricket and went to poetry slams, but Albany's schools were still "inner-city"[2] schools, suffering from the same effects of poverty and divestment that much of upstate New York experienced in the '90s. I asked a lot of "why" questions to make sense of the malaise that I saw—overdoses, brutal fights, and random gang violence, and 77 percent of our high school class dropping out or transferring to "alternative" high schools.

---

2 Paul Beatty's character in *Tuff* was right to ask, "Where is the outer-city?"

My family and the Church answered a lot of those questions. Monday through Friday could have made any kid crazy, but Sunday made sense of it all. On Sunday, I saw all my friends from the suburbs who commuted in to our Vatican II-inspired parish for its celebrated folk music choir and diverse, inclusive parish community. Together, we listened to stories about how Jesus loved us. We knew we could rely on each other, but we had to do Jesus' work for justice in the world if we wanted things to get better.

Being in that community and hearing that message jibed with what I learned from Barbara's story about what "Church" means. Her spirit let me know that at least my compass was pointing in the right direction. The world was crazy and messy, but if the Church stuck together we'd get through it, and even find love and beauty. It didn't all have to make sense; but we did have to find hope in each other.

By the time I graduated high school, I knew I wanted to live a justice-centered life, so I found a university that promised to make me "a man for others." My first day on campus at a major Catholic university was a huge culture shock. On paper, I was an Irish-Catholic academic over-achiever who fit right in, but I had never experienced anything like this in Albany. When I stepped onto campus, I couldn't help wondering, *Where did all these white people come from?*

It wasn't just the complexion of the campus community that was different from my hometown. I remember the first time another student called me a "social-justice Catholic"—was there another kind of Catholic? In college, I met a lot of people who seemed overly concerned with fitting their lived experiences into neat little theological boxes, disregarding how their razor-sharp dividing lines were slicing up living, breathing human beings.

At that university, I learned that there were different levels of Hell that matched exactly how evil you had been in life, and that abortion had always been outlawed but the death penalty was up for debate because it wasn't dogmatically banned, and how important the three words "begotten not made" are to our faith; but I stagnated emotionally and spiritually.

I stopped going to Mass because it seemed like everybody shared an unspoken goal to get out of there as quickly as possible and get back to studying, or drinking, or watching *Lost*. (Once, a priest asked for compliments on the brevity of his homily!) Even when I went on a service trip to North Carolina or an immersion trip to Mexico, I couldn't break out of a worldview that wanted to categorize everything—left or right, right or wrong, girlfriend or friend with benefits. So while I learned and had fun and drank a lot of beer, I was pouring more and more intellectual dirt into the hole where I buried my memories of Barbara and the emotions that her story brought up. I still asked questions, but I lost touch with the instincts that made it possible to know when to take action without needing to have all the answers.

Just when I was thinking the Church was basically irrelevant, the full force of its significance hit me. I returned from study abroad only days before my senior year started, and when I got back to campus I was thrown into the middle of a controversy that had been raging almost since the day I left. Busy finding clubs and *biergärten* in Berlin, I hadn't been paying attention when the university administration decided to give an honorary degree to a top member of President Bush's cabinet, one of the cheerleaders of the Iraq War.

A group of students and teachers protested the graduation ceremonies, sparking a backlash. Then, students were targeted in a series of hate crimes: The Jewish and black student organizations' offices were defaced with swastikas, and a gay freshman's dorm room was vandalized and his possessions destroyed.

I'm not sure how related all of these events were, but things on campus were tense when I returned. During a football game in early October, a group of white dorm-mates attacked three black sophomore women, and tensions at the school rose to the boiling point.

The Campus Police Department failed to classify any of these incidents as hate crimes, and the administration didn't handle the situation with much transparency. Their primary concern appeared to be maintaining the school's prestigious reputation. Many felt that the administration was protecting bigots, and that was enough of a spark to rekindle the flames of discontent that had been smoldering among gay students, female students, and students of color for years.

With a group of my peers, I helped launch a student organization that sought to expose a side of campus life the institution had tried to suppress. We organized students to demand a campus-wide discussion around equity, race, gender, and sexuality, demanding protections for LGBTQ students in the school's non-discrimination policy and a standardized hate-crime protocol. We also pushed to allow students to earn graduation credits studying the history courses most relevant to them, not just American and European political history.

Organizing was hard work, and it left me very tired and angry, but it was also exciting. We built an alternative vision of what our community could be while tackling problems together and supporting each other. I reflect almost daily on the leaders of that campus movement and the time I spent as a member of its ranks.

The administration's failure to address our initial demands kept me organizing throughout my senior year. The president wouldn't call an assembly to openly discuss the deep divisions amongst the student body, so we organized a 1,500-student walkout and rally that took over the middle of campus. Our demand? A university-wide dialogue. Although the school's president wouldn't come out to address the students, he did find the time to pen an Op-Ed to the Boston *Globe* opposing the state's legalization of same-sex marriage.

The university administration finally agreed to change its non-discrimination policy. But instead of including protections for LGBTQ students, the administration simply watered down the whole policy so that it no longer protected anybody. They also tried to intimidate student leaders. I was called into the dean's office after I wrote an article in the school paper criticizing the administration, and we learned that administrators had read our emails when we sent them through the school's servers.

The university defended itself by saying that giving just treatment to students of color, gay students, and women would be in conflict with its "Catholic tradition." This epitomized everything that had come to disappoint and disgust me within the Catholic Church. The university had become yet another place where the Church emphasized policy over pastoral care. Much of the guilt rested with the Board of Trustees, which was seeking to protect a set of financial and political relationships it had worked very hard to build, but most of my companions placed the blame on the entire institutional Church, totally writing Catholicism off.

God had given me a great gift in this conflict, because even as my peers talked about how much they hated the Church, I knew I still loved it. It was ultimately through the conflict with the institutional Church hierarchy that I reconnected with everything I loved about the Catholic community. I began to uncover my memories of Barbara, and all the other events of my childhood, when I finally learned through experience what a loving Church meant.

I knew that God didn't care about categories and boxes and "us versus them." God cared about our love for each other, and God gave me righteous indignation. I started to feel the same anger I felt when I'd first realized that those with power wasted time wondering whether they should help, when any third-grader could tell them, "We have to do something about this!"

As my year of battle wound down, my advisor and mentors encouraged me to apply for a Fulbright Scholarship. I had just wrapped up a 270-page senior thesis and was preparing to return to Europe and pursue a life in academia. But my reconciliation with the Church and God was pushing me in another direction.

I couldn't just write about other people's struggles for justice; I had to go out and make my own history.

The day before graduation, my grandfather died. He was a staunch union man who once risked imprisonment for threatening a strike when New York City wanted to make drastic cuts to the Fire Department. He taught me to always support the union and never to cross a picket line. He loved that I was going to become a history professor, a job he had wanted but never had enough education for before he went into the Navy and then the FDNY. I wanted to make him proud—but his death freed me from concrete expectations of what that meant.

After my grandfather passed away, I realized that I couldn't read books for the rest of my life. I had to *get things done*, as he had. There were so many stories like Barbara's that required us to take action, not study and debate. I couldn't just write about other people's struggles for justice; I had to go out and make my own history.

I applied for the Jesuit Volunteer Corps and headed west to Los Angeles, where JVC placed me with a community-organizing group called People

Organized for Westside Renewal (POWER). At POWER I learned what organizing was, and that I could actually make a living fighting for justice. I knew, immediately, instinctively, that I was in the right place.

I probably could have spent 100 years at college with my head in a book, and I never would have learned about organizing. I could have learned all of Aquinas' theology, and all the doctors of the Church, but I never would have learned what God was really about. I would have spent my whole life in my head. To find God, I had to go down into my heart…and into my gut. I had to dig up my memories of Barbara and the instincts for justice she helped create in me.

When I was a child, the Church taught me that our loving relationships could help heal a cruel world. As a young adult, the Church taught me that its own institutions could be part of that cruelty, but also that oppression creates space for loving resistance. The institutional Church inadvertently taught me that I couldn't sit around and think my way out of problems. I needed to follow my instincts and take *action*.

I needed to knock on doors and build relationships with undocumented immigrants, low-income tenants, LGBTQ youth, and others fighting back against global and local injustices. I needed to bring people together to design actions to win their campaigns. I needed to learn about compromise and accountability. I needed to start trusting that my compass would keep pointing in the right direction and let God decide what the road would look like. I needed to make my life a testament to Barbara's story, which reminds me that even a third-grader knows what justice looks like, while a delusional or jaded adult can accept injustice.

Chasing a Dream in a Foreign Land

Magalí Cecilia
Del Bueno

She held on tightly to her stuffed Mickey Mouse. At three years old, she didn't understand what was happening. The place looked somewhat familiar, and she heard her mother say *aeropuerto* and *avión* to the family surrounding them. A trip! Disneyland again? She loved Disneyland when she visited the year before. Although she remembered feeling restless on the eighteen-hour flight from Buenos Aires, it would be worth it if she was going to see Mickey. But something was different this time. Mom was crying. Her family looked sad. Her grandparents kissed her goodbye, and she smiled as they hugged her with all their might.

What she didn't yet understand was that this would be a permanent relocation to the country of the Happiest Place on Earth. This was the beginning of her immigrant journey.

That little girl was me. My own experiences as an immigrant have given me a deep sense of every person's dignity, as well as a desire to accompany others.

It is hard to explain the distinct sense of living between two worlds that I feel as an immigrant. I spend most of every year studying and working in the United States, where I am a naturalized citizen. The U.S. is my adopted home, the place where I went to school, became engaged in working for justice through my faith, and discovered my love for theology. It is where I will teach the generations to come. My mom and friends in the U.S. help me feel rooted far from my homeland. When summer arrives, however, I'm transported to Argentina and overwhelmed with a sense of history among my family that is missing in the U.S. In Argentina, I feel distinctly American. I speak to my family and friends about my life in California with enthusiasm, and anyone can see the gratitude I feel for my adopted home. At the same time, whenever I leave Argentina, I feel a deep, inexplicable sadness. That sensation also appears when I hear my grandparents' voices, listen to a tango, or speak Spanish in my Argentine accent. In either country, my other home pulls at my heartstrings. This is my life "in-between."

I began to embrace going back and forth between my homes by understanding that I can be a bridge between cultures, languages, and experiences.

I began to embrace going back and forth between my homes by understanding that I can be a bridge between cultures, languages, and experiences, and that I can contribute to greater unity among human beings. In being this bridge, I sought and found God. When I began to encounter undocumented immigrants in my ministries, I imagined not being able to see my family and birth culture, of being eternally isolated from this large part of my life. Through this realization and my deep faith that God creates a positive purpose for each experience, I felt called to be a witness on behalf of other immigrants.

This desire led me to join service trips to Tijuana through Loyola Marymount University (LMU) in Los Angeles. In these volunteer experiences, I'm not just mixing cement to build homes and forming valuable friendships, but I am also putting faces to the immigration debate. At Casa del Migrante, I've shared dozens of meals with migrant men who are waiting to cross into the U.S. or who have recently been deported. Casa offers a free place for up to 180 migrant men to stay.

The conversations, either in Spanish or English, frequently begin with the same questions: "What brings you here? And why are you covered in cement?" As I explain our trip, I often receive words of gratitude. I instantly feel connected to the men because of the in-between feeling we share as migrants, even though our lives are very different. One evening, I noticed a man who was especially quiet at the start of dinner. I smiled at him and we exchanged names. Germán told me that he was from Oaxaca, but that he'd lived in California for twenty years doing painting and construction work. He had been deported on that very day.

When I told him I was studying theology, his eyes lit up and his voice elevated with excitement. "I read books about theology and philosophy! I love learning about life and thinking about complex things. Tell me," he said as he leaned in, "have you heard of Søren Kierkegaard?"

My smile widened. "Yes, I have!"

As Germán shared his fascination, I quickly realized that he knew much more about Kierkegaard than I did. In the middle of what might seem like a difficult conversation, Germán and I had connected. I was philosophizing with him as if we had been friends for years.

"You know what I believe?" Germán continued. "I believe God has a plan for me, like the Bible says in Jeremiah. As hard as it is that my family is in the U.S. and I'm here, I know things will work out. They always do. You know, I got pulled over a few days ago because I was speeding. Now I find myself here in my birth country. Though I love México, I have a life in Santa Ana, a wife and three kids. Want to see them?"

Germán pulled out a tattered wallet with nothing inside but four pictures. "This is Melinda, she's eight. That's Germán, he's six. And Yulia, she's three. And that's all of us with my wife, Sandra. I asked the officers who took me to let me keep the wallet for my pictures. I'm really glad they did. When they dropped me off at the border in Tijuana, I saw a booth with information about Casa. That's how I got here. Like I told you, God was looking out for me."

Another time, I sat with twenty-two-year-old Francisco, as well as Juan, Juan, Juan, and Juan. We all laughed at the abundance of Juans, and Francisco began the conversation with an enthusiasm and positivity we all could feel.

"Let me tell you why I want to go to the United States," Francisco said. "Look at my hand." He held up his right hand, which was missing four fingers. "Ten months ago, I was working in the factory in my hometown in the state of Hidalgo. I was using the machine we call 'the compressor.' I put the piece in, a big block of metal comes down to compress it, and I take the piece out, and so on. Well, this time when I put the piece in, the compressor did its job, but the safety latch, which stops the metal block from coming down when I'm taking the piece out, failed. So as I was pulling it out…SLAM!"

The four Juans and I jumped back as Francisco reenacted what had happened to his hand.

"You know what the funny part is?" Francisco continued. "I didn't feel anything. I could see the blood coming out from under the block and I did scream out of fear, but I felt no pain. Unfortunately, my fingers were severed right off. The doctors couldn't save them. My boss offered me ten thousand pesos for the accident, but also told me that I couldn't keep my job. Ten thousand pesos! That's all my right hand was worth to him."

Ten thousand Mexican pesos are only about eight hundred U.S. dollars.

"You know what, though? I can manage without my other four fingers. I'm just very grateful that I didn't lose my thumb! I wouldn't be able to use a fork the way I can now." Francisco proudly demonstrated his ability to use a fork with his right thumb and what remained of his hand. The four Juans and I were silent, admiring Francisco's efforts. "That's why I want to go to the United States," he explained. "I believe the U.S. treats workers better, and maybe I can make enough money to send back to my wife who lives in México. We just had a baby, so we really need the money. I really hope I make it across and find a job."

At the end of dinner, I said goodbye to Francisco, wished him well on the long journey ahead, and hoped that his dream on the other side of the fence would come true. As I walked away, he gave me an all-American thumbs up with his right hand and we both laughed. Just like every conversation at Casa, I ended this one with a prayer.

Then there was Fernando. As we shared the primary details of our lives—name, hometown, favorite soccer team—Fernando told me that he had gotten very close to becoming a permanent resident of the U.S. "I hired an immigration lawyer, and everything was going well," he said. "He told me I was going to be up for residency soon. I kept on waiting and wasn't called back for months. When I finally reached my lawyer again, he told me my case had been denied. I hadn't committed any crimes, not even a traffic violation. I kept on insisting that my case be fixed, but the lawyer ended up keeping the money I had paid him and told me my case had no hope. When I looked elsewhere for help, I found out there are some immigration lawyers who promise residency to their clients and, when one client has a date to get the residency, they switch that client's file with another person's for more money. So according to the U.S. courts, I have a record of crimes that I have never committed."

> I see the many people who leave their home countries in search of a more just life as my own sisters and brothers.

Fernando paused with a look of confusion, as if he was in disbelief that something like this could happen. "What's worse," he continued, "is that my father got very sick with cancer in Michoacán. I couldn't stay in Los Angeles knowing that my father was dying, so I left and didn't have time to resolve this problem. My father is now better, thank God, and I'm here to try to return to the United States to become a permanent resident. I want to do things legally. I don't understand how this could have happened, but I'm determined to fix it."

The image of Mary and Joseph and Jesus migrating to Egypt comes to my mind at such times, and I wonder why God placed me in front of each man to hear his story. With each encounter, I learn more about my own identity as an immigrant and my own history as I answer their questions about my experiences. This has led me to see the many people who leave their home countries in search of a more just life as my own sisters and brothers, whether I meet them in Mexico, the U.S., or anywhere else.

I bring this deeper understanding back to the U.S., where I don't need to look far to find stories such as those of Germán, Francisco, and Fernando.

A few years ago, I discovered one of my closest friends, Ezequiel, looking pensively at a holy card he always carried in his pocket. When I asked him about it, he said, "The holy card belonged to my grandfather, who died two years ago. I couldn't say goodbye to him when he was dying in Guatemala." Ezequiel's eyes filled with tears.

My own eyes welled up as I thought about my grandparents in Argentina and felt the all-too-familiar sadness. Ezequiel continued, "I couldn't go because I'm undocumented, Magalí. I've been so afraid to say it, but I'm starting to let more friends know because I can't do this alone. It's hard, but I believe God has a plan for this."

My sadness turned into gratitude that Ezequiel trusted me to share the hardship with which he lives each day. Much later, he told me, "Through your kinship I'm able to experience God's support, trust, and love on a different level because you *literally* walk *with me* in my times of need. I knew I really wasn't alone and felt God's support, trust, and love through you. I became empowered and have gathered the courage to become more proactive on immigration issues."

And let me tell you, a beautiful thing about kinship is that it is reciprocal. Ezequiel and the others like him who have touched my life have truly allowed me to find God in all people and situations.

After learning Ezequiel's story, I began working with undocumented students whose journeys to college are often filled with uncertainty. Many students only realize they're undocumented for the first time when applying to college. They know they were not born in the U.S., but until they are asked for "proper documentation" by a school, they might not know the full extent of what being undocumented means. They must then undergo the difficult task of identifying universities that accept and support them. Without knowing that many universities do this, students might apply only to community colleges and state schools, sometimes truncating their full potential. Undocumented students do not qualify for many federal and state scholarships and loans, no matter how strong their academic records, and must rely heavily on the generosity of universities and external private scholarships to help them afford their studies. Imagine how frustrating it is to hear from administrators, "Well, you're an amazing student and would excel at our school, but we *can't* offer you any financial help." (Or they *won't*.)

Those students who are not completely discouraged might still find ways to pay for school, usually working forty-plus hours a week while studying full-time, commuting from home, or taking out one of the few high-interest loans available to them. The family also helps by taking out a second mortgage on their home, for example, in the rare case that they own a home. Once they begin college, these students go through their years—usually more than four—discerning whom they can trust with their secret. Those fortunate enough to graduate find that many employers will not hire them and do not value their achievements because they remain undocumented. These students are fully prepared to run the race toward their dreams, but their feet have been glued to the ground.

The undocumented students at LMU told me I could help just by sharing their stories. Given that my peers may risk deportation if they identify themselves as undocumented, they gave me the honor of reading their written, anonymous testimonies to the university community on various occasions. Juxtaposing fear and hope, these stories speak of their unique struggles. One young woman shared her dreams that are wrapped in uneasiness.

The connection formed with others when I share their testimonies is a catalyst for true social change.

"If I am able to graduate from Loyola Marymount's undergraduate program," she told me, "my future will remain uncertain. I am not sure I will even have a job after graduation. I can only hope that more people become aware of what undocumented students have to offer, and what we go through. We are just like any other student with hopes and aspirations, except for the fact that our future, along with our accomplishments, is subject to the generosity and determination of others who advocate for us. We are invisible."

These young people shared their stories to encourage broader understanding for the many students and their families who can no longer remain invisible. Ezequiel believes that the connection formed with others when I share their testimonies is a catalyst for true social change, because "when one has deep faith in God and experiences true kinship, one witnesses a deeper level of empowerment and solidarity." This is why I will continue to speak for those who cannot speak freely and will advocate for undocumented youth seeking more opportunities to fulfill their dreams of education.

Legislation to help undocumented students obtain educational funding has been proposed throughout the U.S. Nevertheless, it is often hindered by anti-immigrant sentiment that crosses party lines. I hope that somehow and someday, through the understanding of the lives of these invisible students who bravely share their stories with me and other supporters, negative attitudes toward immigrants will become a thing of the past and higher education will become more accessible to all students, regardless of immigrant status. At the center of the debates about immigration lies the well-being of fellow human beings, which is sometimes forgotten in today's political power battles.

I continue to search for ways to minister to and support my sisters and brothers who come to the U.S. in search of a better life, as my family did. My experience as an immigrant gives me the energy and continued desire to accompany others. God has led me to cross paths with these beautiful people, and as a pilgrim in the Catholic Church I will continue to work for justice, responding to Jesus' example of standing with the "least" in society, who are truly the greatest in the Kingdom of God.

Gaining My Moral Compass

Justin Sengstock

On Tuesday of Holy Week 2011, I spent a wet hour-and-a-half out-side Chicago's Holy Name Cathedral with about fifty other people. I carried a sign with a paraphrase of Galatians 3:28: "There is neither male nor female. In Christ Jesus you all are one." We were protesting for women's ordination, standing where the lines of priests processing inside for the annual Chrism Mass had no choice but to see and hear us.

I was there because I volunteered with Call To Action, a progressive Catholic reform organization headquartered in Chicago, whose staff I have since joined. We advocate for women priests, married priests, bishop accountability, gay rights, and an emphasis on love rather than doctrine (among many other things). We seek a just, inclusive Church.

I noted the reactions of the priests as they entered the big yellow-stone cathedral. Some had been chatting on their way out of the neighboring school building, and they pointedly kept chatting. Some smiled politely; a handful graciously accepted our fliers. One murmured his sympathy and shrugged.

But a few couldn't contain their opposition. One shook his head at us impatiently. Another waved his finger at us like we were naughty children and said, with self-confidence that made me wince, that we should work on filling up all the empty convents.

Not long ago, I was just like them. I, too, would have sat in judgment over those who called for a more inclusive Church. You see, I had once been a very conservative, card-carrying member of the "JP2, We Love You" crowd.

I was not raised that way. My parents were not overly religious, although my dad became a devout Lutheran later in life. But I picked up religion as a teen, probably because I hadn't grown up around very much of it. It was a define-my-own-identity thing—other teenagers cussed and avoided curfew and steamed up the windows of cars making out. I prayed in Latin and wanted to know everything the pope ever said.

I was obsessed with popes. By the time I was in high school, I had memorized all the popes from St. Peter down to John Paul II, their names and dates in office. During my first year at Loyola University Chicago, after reading an article in the student paper arguing that intellectual inquiry was a main Jesuit charism, I fired back a letter to the editor explaining that obeying the pope was more important. I majored in theology, vaguely expecting a teaching career in which I would promote more of this sort of thing.

But even in my first year of college, my hyper-Catholicism was already on its way out. I was becoming tired, sensing emptiness. Religion had become years of discipline and obedience, doing things just because I was supposed to do them. I shook inside when I finally understood none of this had brought me peace. I resisted the insight, but it wouldn't go away.

I don't know where my faith would have ended up without a major intervention. What brought about that intervention was that I needed friends.

I'm an only child, and a shy one. Catholicism was, in part, a refuge: most people had other people, but I had God. I did make a few friends by the end of high school, but as of my sophomore year in college, I was basically back on my own. I didn't even have a roommate.

So I started hunting for people the only way I knew. I hovered at the edges of university ministry, attending a retreat here and there. Maybe my social life and my piety would perk up together. I still had hope for my piety.

On one of those retreats I met a girl who lived in Agape House, an intentional community run through the ministry department. I immediately remembered the name and caught the reference. The previous winter, I had seen yellow fliers at Mass in Loyola's chapel, advertising a living environment built around the pillars of spirituality, justice, simple living, and community.

I had experienced momentary intrigue. I took a flier back to my dorm, where I read that I would have to commit to six hours of some kind of service work per week. With that, I threw it away. As a busy slave of my grade-point average, I refused to do six more hours a week of anything.

But, one winter later, the service work did not seem like an obstacle. I was glad to be reminded of Agape. I was done with wandering campus unattached.

In filling out the application, I was almost stymied by the requirement that I submit a recent photo of myself. That was how few people I had around me. I seriously wondered who would take it. In the end, my generous R.A. took the picture, in which I wore too much hair gel.

I dropped the package at the ministry building and slid neatly through the interview a week later. When I got the call that I was in, I felt very proud. I didn't feel quite so proud when I learned later that the number of spots and the number of applicants had been the same.

I wasn't sure what to expect in August 2003 when, now a junior, I moved into my room on the dorm floor that Agape House occupied. I had met the other members all of twice. And I did remember the mysterious remark my friend from the retreat had made when I told her I was applying: "Don't expect anything, because whatever you think it's going to be, it's not."

But I guess I did expect something. My only other experience with people my age in a spiritual environment was in carefully controlled situations, like retreats or diocesan youth conferences. That led me to fondly suspect that I would bond with folks very like myself who would help me rebuild my shaky certainties.

Oops.

Just the externals told me I was living in a whole new world. I had standards of cleanliness that would be the envy of TV detective Adrian Monk, but I was suddenly stepping over piles of laundry and smelly shoes. I sighed at our community room, always overrun with used mugs and spoons, an ongoing flow of relics from my new housemates, who drank tea with an almost hysterical insistency.

There was the night I was astonished to hear one housemate ask, "Okay, show of hands: who here's a virgin and who's not?" Then there was the meeting where, as we sat sweating in an eighty-degree room with no fan, we took almost an hour to debate what lettuce we should buy and where it was going to come from and whether or not it was going to be organic.

Almost everybody seemed to consider social justice our community's main pillar. Dinner talk was often occupied with ruminations about Latin America and green living. My head swam with odd turns of phrase: Just what was "pedagogy of the oppressed" or "fair-trade coffee"?

For me, the justice pillar was an afterthought. It was simply the price of admission so I wouldn't be alone. In retrospect this is curious, given my near-worship of the popes. Clearly the insights of Leo XIII and Pius XI on economic justice and unions, the teachings of Paul VI on peace and human development, and the commitment of John Paul II to a Polish democratic movement that paralleled liberation theology (though he would not have phrased it that way) had yet to make much impact on me.

Incidentally, nobody shared my awe for the popes. One girl was upfront about her desire to be the first woman priest. She frequently said things like, "God is not a boy's name."

Reeling, I wondered if I had made a big mistake. I think they wondered if I had made a big mistake, too. After all, it is hard to connect with someone who always looks shell-shocked.

But the turning point came right about then. On the balmy night of our excruciating vegetable negotiations, I was wandering the campus in a daze when I ran into one of the Loyola chaplains. I poured out some of my frustrations. She nodded in all the right places, but then she gently pointed out that I had chosen Agape House and that they were now my family.

This jolted me into awareness. I realized I had joined the community to run away from something. But if I was to stay there, I would have to run toward something, or rather somebody—a group of somebodies. I had to decide to be present to my family where they were.

Even so, "presence" is a catchword that can mean anything or nothing. I had just sat with everybody in our house meeting and been utterly disengaged, noting the proceedings like a court reporter but chiefly interested in the ticking minutes on my watch. So what is presence when you make it a verb?

I decided that, for me, presence meant listening. I wasn't a talker who could find something to say to everybody about anything at any time. I wasn't an instinctive caretaker, knowing exactly when to give people hugs or make them bowls of soup. But I could make a discipline of hearing everything everybody ever said and sitting on it before reacting to it.

The result was an interpersonal revolution. I woke up to find myself having real conversations, with people my age, on a consistent basis, for the first time in my life. They were confiding things to me. This had rarely happened in the preceding twenty years. It was as if my housemates could tell the hour of my about-face.

I woke up to find myself having real conversations, with people my age, on a consistent basis, for the first time in my life.

And in this context, I became ready for a spiritual revolution. Much of what I was listening to was about how the Catholic Church, which had given me so much of my identity, had both inspired and betrayed the formerly strange housemates who were becoming my friends.

One night, the girl who wanted to be ordained announced she was going to RSVP for a Jesuit vocations retreat. She typed out the email right there in the community room as we watched. She knew, of course, that they would refuse her.

Lo and behold, the next night she was back in the community room, reading aloud the expected Jesuit response: She needed other weekend plans. I wondered why she had bothered. And up to that moment, I still thought priests should be men.

But I had come to respect this feisty woman who had a laser-eyed B.S.

detector that would not let me get away with anything. I was fast learning to measure whatever I said around her to ensure it made sense. And when she felt strongly enough about something to make a dramatic, apparently useless gesture, I suddenly needed to measure my own feelings, too.

I started to wonder if God is really so rigid and linear about who does what. Would God really be more unsympathetic and exclusionary than I had the guts to be, now that I realized "heretics" had faces and names and lived with me? My responses at Mass began creeping toward a genderless format: "for us and for our salvation"; "it is right to give God thanks and praise."

Another housemate was, at the time, agnostic. He spoke about the moment that defined his attitude: His best friend from high school had died one night from an asthma attack. His inhaler had been only a few inches out of his frantic reach when he lost consciousness. Life seemed random, the universe morally neutral, and God absent.

Would God really be more unsympathetic and exclusionary than I had the guts to be, now that I realized "heretics" had faces and names and lived with me?

I realized my own historic comfort with the Catholic system, which purported to explain in detail everything that God could possibly do or want, was the product of luck. Senseless death was simply not a part of my personal experience. It was easy for me to recite the answers when I didn't have to live the questions. Maybe it was equally easy for buffered, insulated clergy who lived downtown or in the Vatican.

But perhaps the biggest influences on me were two other housemates. One was an anthropology major who kept a faux hominid skull in his room. The other was a fellow theology major, a girl who used a Fritz Eichenberg print of Jesus in a soup line as her laptop wallpaper. When they weren't spending time with us, or doing their homework at the last possible minute, they always seemed to be off working at homeless shelters somewhere. And even at their busiest, they both still had something to give to everybody, a feat I have never managed.

Watching them in action convinced me that religion had no inherent meaning in the ways in which I was accustomed to using it, as a kind of spiritual club and intellectual hobby. Abandoned people cannot feel your prayers and do not wish to meditate on your theology, but they do warm up when you treat them with dignity. This is true for the abandoned cast onto our streets. This is true for the abandoned cast out of our pews. My Catholicism, to have any relevance, would depend less on what I believed than on what I did, and for whom.

There were other lessons that year. Hanging out with my community members and their friends, I had my first conscious encounters with people who were gay and lesbian. I am embarrassed to admit my astonishment that they were not the anti-life, hedonistic cabal that the Catholic hierarchy darkly suggested they were. When I began accepting that a guy kissing a guy or a woman kissing a woman was not disruptive to the fabric of reality, I wondered if I was losing my moral compass. I now know I was actually gaining it.

With the rest of Agape House, I also went to my first protest, the annual demonstration at the School of the Americas (now WHINSEC) in Fort Benning, Georgia. Here, the U.S. government trains soldiers who serve repressive regimes in Latin America. Holding my white cross in memory of murdered thousands, I got over my image of protesters as long-ago hippies who needed to air out their VW buses. I also got over my self-image as a "respectable" person who, because of my respectability, didn't "do things like that." It was immersion therapy, and good training for my work today.

Even these lessons were but commentary on what I was learning at my new home, fulfilling my commitment to listen to everything. In a sense, the Agape community room replaced Loyola as my university that year. Here I learned what I could only understand when I sat at the margins of the Church instead of in its grand, baroque center. And here was my adopted family.

Our year ended. We disbanded, graduated, moved on. For the first few years after college, I was mostly interested in getting a job that would pay enough so that I could move out of my parents' house and stay out. But the economy made it painfully clear that my goal would be elusive no matter what career I chose.

So I started thinking less about my personal prosperity and living situation, and I focused instead on what I wanted my work to mean. I remembered my adopted family. I remembered the Church at the margins.

In summer 2010, I attended a "Mary Magdalene service," a prayer service honoring female leadership in the Catholic Church throughout the ages. Afterward, I noticed an older gentleman tabling for Call To Action. I knew about their Church reform work, since one of my Loyola friends used to coordinate their young adult program.

I sensed this was the time I would either stand up for what mattered to me or not. I strode over to the man at the table and the first words out of my mouth were, "So, do you need volunteers?" His eyes popped a little at my abrupt introduction.

Two weeks later he was my boss.

I would lie if I said the work of Catholic reform is perpetually exciting. I have learned far more about spreadsheets and databases and online banking than I ever wanted to know. But if you do not take care of the practical and the mundane, you have no network to gather the people.

And spreadsheets are not all I do. I have written prayer services for Call To Action chapter meetings. I helped develop a Stations of the Cross service that reflects on issues of Church justice. I am incessantly tapping out posts for Young Adult Catholics, our outreach blog for people in their 20s and 30s.

Then there are moments when it all takes flesh, like on the steps of Holy Name Cathedral. Despite the raw weather, I relished the chance to prove, once and for all, that I finally understood God wasn't a boy's name.

In his "Letter to a Young Activist," Thomas Merton wrote that "gradually you struggle less and less for an idea and more and more for specific people. The range tends to narrow down, but it gets much more real. In the end, it is the reality of personal relationships that saves everything."

Yes.

The Scandal of Our Tradition

Katherine Schmidt

I began college with visions of protests dancing in my head. Cautionary tales from high school teachers about the evils of liberal higher education—tales that, incidentally, only whetted my growing appetite to challenge unjust systems—created my image of college as a place of activism and revolution. But instead, I found complacent teenagers at a small, liberal arts Catholic college in the mountains, seemingly unaware of American wars being fought on dubious premises and annoyed by talk of current events. Although some students shared my concern for the injustices happening in the off-campus world, I struggled to find a place for my youthful activist passion within the community of affluent, entitled kids I had unwittingly joined.

I found my solace in theology and chose it as my major after studying Catholic social teaching. My desire for social action, however unfortunately imbued with romantic scenes of Vietnam-era protests, only grew as I acquired theological grounding in the Church's social encyclicals. I became energized by the consistent ethic of life, the idea that being "pro-life" encompassed much more than just opposing abortion. Social teaching that addressed the question of justice for all people became the center of my personal and academic life. One issue that seemed particularly under-examined was the death penalty. Though I had attended a few execution vigils in high school, my first opportunity for real activism arrived when a philosophy professor held a meeting for students interested in abolishing the death penalty in Maryland and beyond. Thus began my time as a death penalty abolitionist.

Our first campus meeting of the Campaign to End the Death Penalty (CEDP) started strong, attracting about twenty students, a respectable number for a college of less than two thousand. In the first few months, we hosted several speakers and events that piqued the interest of the student body. Faculty encouraged their students to attend our events, and some even spoke from their professional perspectives about the issue.

One of our earliest events featured two men who had been exonerated from death row. The room was jam-packed with students, held unusually rapt by the tragic stories of the men before them. Another event, a panel of experts offering perspectives on the death penalty, drew a standing-room-only crowd, which made me giddy with a feeling of palpable, forward-moving energy. In those early days, we felt we were stirring the campus as a whole, beyond our personal acquaintances, to a greater awareness of the injustice of capital punishment. We hoped this awareness would lead to great results in the form of activism and change, especially to foster public voting will to end the death penalty in Maryland.

The following year, I agreed to be vice president of CEDP, with my dear friend Sarah as president. We quickly realized that our chapter was not as strong as it had been. We gained a few new members but remained a smaller version of our earlier self. What I remember most clearly from that year was our extensive effort at "tabling." On our small campus, almost every student—and most faculty—ate lunch and dinner in the same place. Equipped with extensive research on the social, racial, moral, and financial aspects of the death penalty, our organization began an information campaign during meals. Specifically, we wanted to combat the common arguments in favor of capital punishment. For example, for lunch and dinner one day, we handed out big, brightly colored dollar bills with the governor's face on them. Where the denomination would be, we had placed "$2 million"—the amount that the state of Maryland actually spends on court costs per case to put a person to death. We wanted to counter the myth that it costs less to put a person to death than to keep someone in prison for life.

It was through my experience "tabling" that I first realized the challenge of abolition work. One particularly slow night in the cafeteria, I went from table to table with my information sheets. On many campuses, this might be seen as immensely awkward or rude, but I determined that our school was just small enough that it might work—although I didn't know exactly what success would look like.

"Hi, guys. We're distributing some information about the death penalty," I began.

Silence. Stunned faces.

"I was wondering what you all thought about the issue, or if I could answer any questions…." I trailed off, hoping someone would chime in.

People did not want to look past their knee-jerk, emotional reactions and actually talk about the death penalty.

"No questions," a male student said. "If you kill someone, you need to be killed."

His friends nodded.

I tried my best to respond. "Well, what about forgiveness? We're at a Catholic school, and a cornerstone of the faith is forgiveness."

"All right, whatever."

I had prepared myself for awkward conversations, but I had not expected utter disengagement. Time and again, mention of the Catholic Church brought the conversation to a screeching halt. In fairness, however, most of my talking points did. People did not want to look past their knee-jerk, emotional reactions and actually talk about the death penalty. At least one person at any given table would be looking at her food, her lap, the floor—anything that could distract her from the conversation. I had expected long discussions about the morality of the death penalty. The energy of the year before had belied a real and serious fact: getting people, especially young people, to engage in the capital punishment discussion was the first and most difficult task at hand.

Although encountering so much complacency discouraged me, it also better prepared me for the work. And other times, I encountered folks who needed no prompting to engage the topic of capital punishment. One summer afternoon, my sister and I were leaving the beach when a middle-aged man approached us.

"You don't actually believe that, do you?" he said, gesturing toward the bumper sticker on my car.

In yellow letters on a black background, it read: THE DEATH PENALTY IS A HATE CRIME.

"Well," I started, "yes, sir. Yes, I do."

He wasted no time launching into one of the most common arguments: "Would you feel that way if your mother was murdered?"

"I can't say how I'd feel," I admitted, "but my faith compels me to love all people. I believe that people are more than their greatest sins, even if those sins were committed against my family."

"Well, I think you'll change your mind when you're older," he said.

"I hope not, because that would mean I had lost my faith in Christ," I answered.

His face changed from a scowl to a smirk. "Okay, what denomination are you?"

Since we were in southern Virginia, I quickly assumed that he was probably Southern Baptist and would dismiss my views and chalk them up to differences among traditions when he found out I was Catholic.

"Well, sir," I said, and then paused. "I'm Catholic."

His face fell immediately, and his voice grew quiet when he answered, "So am I."

My heart raced as I reminded him of our Church's teaching on the death penalty. He looked down at his feet. He explained that he had always struggled with the Church's position on capital punishment because he didn't know how he could forgive someone if a member of his family had been murdered.

While this encounter reminded me of the difficulty of turning even those within my own Church against capital punishment, I left hopeful. I knew that I had at least made one more person, one more Christian, think about the implications of his faith regarding the fact that our government kills other human beings and calls it justice.

Once again, I found myself in the campus cafeteria promoting a panel of murder victims' families. I stood up to greet a mass of men leaving the cafeteria, all dressed in black and chatting quietly to each other. They were members of the diocesan seminary attached to my college. The seminarians were mostly detached from the activities of the college, with the exception of meals and philosophy classes. As a philosophy minor, I had come to know some of the "men in black."

The stream of seminarians ignored my advertising of the evening's event. I stopped one of my classmates near the end of the pack, a first-year seminarian.

"Hey, you guys should come tonight."

"Oh, I think we're pretty busy tonight," he replied.

I decided to just ask.

"Listen, why is it that you guys don't seem to support our work?" Hoping to find some common ground, I offered, "I mean, John Paul II has been pretty clear about the death penalty."

"Yeah, definitely," he agreed. "I just think that most of us feel like abortion is the more pressing issue. Because, you know, there are millions of babies being killed."

In that moment, I clearly felt the optimism drain from my heart. I suppose I always knew that some people stratified life issues in their minds, but never had it been made so painfully obvious. This particular argument struck me as oddly utilitarian, as if the number of abortions somehow trumped the "few" lives of people on death row. Shrouded in the language of strategy or prudence, making distinctions about the value of human life seemed to run contrary to the very tradition of protecting all human life that the Church purports to espouse. I came to realize that the issue of capital punishment brings into sharp relief the struggle at the heart of what it means to be a follower of Christ—namely, the struggle to love those whom it is not easy to love.

That night, I attended the panel of murder victims' family members.

Before it began, I looked around the auditorium with the seminarian's words ringing in my ears. A woman whose seven-year-old daughter had been murdered snapped me out of my frustration and reoriented my focus to the issue at hand.

"I came to a place," she said, "where I realized that God loved [the murderer] as much as he loved my little girl."

Engaging with the issue of capital punishment in any kind of concerted way means opening oneself to some of the greatest tragedies of life.

Engaging with the issue of capital punishment in any kind of concerted way means opening oneself to some of the greatest tragedies of life. I realized that night that I also had the privilege of encountering the fullness of hope and reconciliation through this work, as I witnessed the way this mother embodied the forgiveness of Christ.

One of the last formal events about the death penalty I attended was a conference honoring lawyers, activists, doctors, and clergy for their activism to end capital punishment. My first inclination was to feel small—my letters to death row inmates, campus programming, and efforts to raise awareness felt insignificant compared to these honorees. But that night, I came to believe something that sticks with me to this day. I began to think about the Passion of Jesus. Simon helped carry the very cross of Christ, bearing in his body some of Jesus' physical strife. Veronica, on the other hand, simply wiped Jesus' face, doing what she could to ease his pain.

In any justice movement, there are Simons and there are Veronicas. This past Christmas, I stumbled upon a box of letters from death row inmates. The letters were responses to Christmas cards I had sent out during my senior year of college, a task I had undertaken alone when nearly all of our members stopped showing up to meetings. I read through the letters again and decided to respond. Writing to inmates is a small thing, a mere moment of comfort in a long process of suffering. But if I learned anything as an advocate against capital punishment, it is that we press on. As long as the injustice of the death penalty persists, so too must we persist, often in ways that seem small, insignificant, and consistently futile. Although we will undoubtedly be frustrated by the complacency, opposition, or outright apathy we find in our own Church, we must also remember the scandal of our tradition: We follow a God who was once a victim of capital punishment. Inspired and sustained by the self-giving love of the Cross, in ways small and large, we respond to the call for justice.

Gory Stuff and the Virgin Mary

Johanna Hatch

Thursday, February 23
Clinic escort training. I am simultaneously excited and terrified. I've been trying to make this happen since I moved to the city and discovered that my house is four blocks from a clinic that needs escorts on Saturdays. So now I am sitting in a cozy conference room, surrounded by a group of very nice people, eating Oreos and listening as our facilitator, a bouncy young woman with curly brown hair, tells us what protesters can and can't do. Protestors can say anything they want to you, as long as it doesn't constitute a threat. Apparently, "Burn in hell" does not constitute a threat. Protesters can take your picture to try to intimidate you. You shouldn't say your name or the name of another escort if the protesters are within hearing range; they'll remember it and use it to try to engage you. Whatever you do, don't engage the protesters.

I am trying to focus on what the facilitators are telling me: your job is to create a safe space for the patient in the cacophony of pleas and condemnation. Here comes a piece of literature someone picked up from a protester: "What Clinic Escorts Really Believe." It says that we don't care about women, that we don't want women to know what their options are. Someone asks, "What are the protesters like?"

"There's a couple of regulars, older people," one of the facilitators replies, "and a couple of younger guys. They walk up and down the sidewalk saying Hail Marys. And they bring pictures—the gory stuff—and a giant Virgin Mary statue."

I snicker because it's so stereotypical. But then I look around at the other snickering faces.

Should I tell them I'm Catholic? Or will that make them think I'm somehow more sympathetic to the "other side"? Because my faith is aligned with the political forces that seek to outlaw abortion and contraception, how many people can I tell that I'm Catholic before it will be used against me?

Saturday, April 8
It's 6:30 a.m. and a bit chillier than I had anticipated. As I turn the corner to the clinic, I notice there are no protesters yet. There's just one guy in a huge puffy parka standing on the sidewalk by the front door.

"Do you know if there's clinic today?" he asks.

"I think so," I reply, unsure if he's with the escorts or the protesters. A woman in her thirties with short hair and glasses approaches us.

"Good morning," she says with a smile. "Is our team leader here yet?" The door to the clinic opens and our team leader, a stocky, gray-haired woman, ushers us in. We sit in a conference room with the rest of the escorts. There's a thin girl with glasses, probably about my age, a guy with lip and eyebrow piercings, and another young man with a stocking cap and a huge cup of coffee. I'm surprised by the number of men who have gotten up this early, joking with each other about getting dressed in the dark so they didn't disturb their wives. Later, a friend will ask me about these men: "Do you wonder what their stories are? What led them to be clinic escorts?"

Our team leader divides us into two groups, consisting of three people each, stationed at each entrance to the parking garage where patients park. As we walk to our posts, I spot the first protesters unloading signs from their trunks. As promised, I catch a glimpse of a giant, mutilated fetus.

I am by the parking garage with the two people I met outside. I come to call them Big Coat Guy and ELCA Lady—which I've learned because, inevitably, religion comes up.

Religion is a hard topic to avoid in front of an abortion clinic. Images of Jesus or the Virgin Mary, threats of hell, and promises of God's love or vengeance are common parts of protesters' early-morning scripts. Seminarians walk up and down the block, praying the Rosary. I don't realize how vicious the use of this imagery can be until I see the first patient escorted into the clinic. As the escort walks back to her station, the most vocal—and the only woman—protester produces a bottle of holy water and begins shaking it vigorously in the direction of the escort. I nervously finger my Virgin of Guadalupe necklace but quickly drop my hand. I'm not sure that I want to draw the attention of my fellow escorts to the religious symbol I share with the protestors.

Could we find common ground through our shared religious tradition, or would she see me as a traitor?

After that, whenever one of us walks by with a patient, this protester starts her vocal loop over again: "Your baby wants to live and be adopted! Don't do this! Don't go in there! Your baby doesn't want to be aborted! If you do this, it will haunt you the rest of your life!"

Once the patient is inside, she turns her wrath on the escorts.

"This baby's blood is on your hands! This baby will be on your conscience and you'll see it on your deathbed. God's vengeance is freely given, but you have to beg for God's mercy! You need to get down on your knees and repent and beg God to forgive you!"

I assume that she is a Christian, and judging by the holy water, a Catholic. What would she think if she knew I was also Catholic? Could we find common ground through our shared religious tradition, or would she see me as a traitor?

As a Catholic clinic escort, I experience a range of emotions, but the two strongest are offense and isolation. I am offended that those who protest outside the clinic use treasured symbols of my tradition as weapons to scare, to guilt, and to separate themselves from the escorts, who they see as accomplices to murder. The holy waters of baptism, the prayers my mother prayed for strength and sanity, and the image of our Blessed Mother that comforted me all my life have been hijacked and turned against me.

While my involvement as an escort isolates me from members of my faith, my faith isolates me from my political allies. Although I'm a committed reproductive justice activist, I have had long conversations with many who see my continued participation in the Church as unquestioned allegiance to an organization that continues to oppress women and the GLBT community. Because of this, I never reveal my religious tradition to my fellow clinic escorts.

I have always known that I have been called to walk with women as a companion and advocate in the face of the world's cruelties. In my professional life, I've responded to this calling by working to prevent and address the root causes of sexual assault and working with immigrant, refugee, and battered women. As a volunteer clinic escort, I literally become a shield. I put my body between a woman—making what might be the most difficult choice she will ever make—and images of violence and voices of condemnation. I accompany these women for a brief part of their life journey—promising neither to judge or take any decision away from them, nor to alleviate the burden of their responsibility. I simply offer safe passage.

Saturday, June 17
On this warm, bright June morning, young women, from early college to young professionals, make up the entire escort group. Thanks to the warm weather, the protesters are in full force, including two women I have never seen before. As the first patients arrive, I know that this morning is going to be different than any I've experienced yet.

The first car that pulls into the parking garage has South Dakota plates. The driver is a woman younger than me, and she is alone. She has driven at least seven hours to get here, and it is barely 7:00 a.m. As she crosses the sidewalk, the infinite loop begins: "Please don't kill your baby! Your baby wants to live!"

Since there are more protesters than usual—ten or so compared to the usual three or four—they can focus more energy on the escorts. One woman holds a Rosary and stares at two escorts on the corner, not speaking. The woman who had the holy water last time starts in on my escort partner and me. I don't even hear her words this time. I turn my back to her; I don't have the energy to go on the defensive this early.

As we cross the street with patients, protesters hold out literature to us. The little tract is called, "Why Trust Planned Parenthood?"—even though this clinic is not affiliated with Planned Parenthood. I've already seen this tract at my alma mater. It is filled with inaccuracies and calls being gay, lesbian, bisexual, or transgender a "sexual disorder." *Are they actually changing minds with this?* I wonder.

A poster I have never seen before is on display today: a painting of, well, a pile of fetuses upon which is Jesus on the cross, with Mary on his right and the United States flag at half mast on his left. It is a bizarre juxtaposition of religion and patriotism. What are the protesters attempting to convey to me, using this image? Abortion isn't patriotic, but Jesus is? That they have both a patriotic and spiritual duty to stop abortion?

As more patients arrive, the protesters grow bolder. Escorts dash across the grass to reach patients at their cars before the protesters can rush them on the sidewalk. Protesters challenge the masculinity of male companions: "A real man wouldn't let his girlfriend go in there!"

My involvement as a clinic escort raises the inevitable question: How can I be Catholic and support legal abortion? How can I escort women on their way to having an abortion?

The answers are not simple, nor 100 percent theologically clear. What I do know is that our Church places a high value on the formation of and obedience to one's conscience. The *Catechism of the Catholic Church* states that "conscience is the aboriginal Vicar of Christ."[3] Through a conscience formed by years of first pro-life activism, then a retreat to the wilderness, I came to the conclusion through much listening and study that I could not in good conscience advocate making abortion illegal.

But before that, I spent my high school years marching and rallying against abortion and praying with my youth group. As I entered college, I

---

3 *Catechism of the Catholic Church.* 1778.

began to chafe against the sexual teachings of the Church, my heart broken when my old youth group shunned gay friends and when I learned of the complicity of the hierarchy in the sexual abuse of children. I pulled away, trying to make sense of my faith. I learned that many denominations and traditions support a woman's ability to make her own choices regarding reproduction. As I studied feminist theory, I could not ignore the voices of women who lived in a time when all women were denied the ability to make their own reproductive choices. And in listening to the voices of women who have had abortions, including kind, wise women who also happened to be the mothers of my good friends, I have learned that they are not immoral people who deserve to be shamed or vilified—they are simply people who made the best choice they could, whether pregnancy was forced upon them or whether they faced it while homeless, jobless, or alone. In light of this, my conscience tells me that abortion is a decision each woman must make for herself, that women do not reach this decision lightly, and that women should not be condemned for it. When I returned to the Catholic Church, I could not leave these women and their lives behind.

Writer Lynn Harris, of the Reform Jewish tradition, articulates similar motivations to mine when she describes her service as part of New York City's Haven Coalition, which provides overnight shelter for women who have to travel from out of state for an abortion. She and her husband were motivated by "the Jewish commandments to help and protect our neighbor," and *tzedakah*, "which is not an act of magnanimous charity...but one of justice: giving the poor their due."[4]

I do not believe my work as a clinic escort is particularly special or worthy of praise, nor do I pretend that it is blessed or even accepted by the institutional Roman Catholic Church. I do know, however, that what I do is an act of kindness toward my neighbors who are isolated and marginalized. Because I am the product of a Benedictine education, I offer hospitality and a listening ear. As clinic escort, I am acting on everything I learned about how to be Catholic.

Nonetheless, I occupy a tense, awkward, and creative space, while knowing that, according to the Guttmacher Institute, 27 percent of women who have abortions in the United States describe themselves as Catholic—a

4   Harris, Lynn. "Strangers on the Sofa." *Tablet: A New Read on Jewish Life*. 29 March 2006. Web.

greater percentage than those who identified themselves as having no religious affiliation.[5] Catholics are on both sides of the line, picketing the clinics, working inside, and even seeking abortions. As a clinic escort, I move across and through, transgressing the polarized spaces with the reality of the women who must make the choice often lost between them. I am an emissary, asking questions of both sides: Why is a woman's ability to make her own moral choice offensive to you? What does it say about our society's view of women, not only that many have abortions but also that many must face unplanned pregnancy in the first place? Why do we punish women for their choices, no matter what choice they make? We ostracize women who have abortions even as we fire pregnant teachers from Catholic schools if they are unmarried. Do we put enough energy into protecting the dignity of all women's choices, including raising a child or giving one up for adoption? Do we, as Catholics, really believe that divisive teachings on sex, sexuality, and reproduction are truly God's will for God's people to live in justice and equality?

Do we, as Catholics, really believe that divisive teachings on sex, sexuality, and reproduction are truly God's will for God's people to live in justice and equality?

I don't fit the image of the clinic escort—someone who "promotes abortion" and tries to keep women in the dark—embraced by the protesters, nor am I the caricature of Catholicism that my fellow escorts see in the protestors. I am just a woman attempting to live my faith while not abandoning my conscience, hoping that my presence will open the hearts of those holding the gory signs and the Virgin Mary statues to the clinic escorts, and helping my fellow escorts know that the Catholicism I know is a faith of compassion, justice, and love. I may never reach a satisfactory resolution, but I will wrestle with the hard questions as I inhabit the borderlands of Catholicism and reproductive justice activism, walking always with God's most precious daughters, even across a picket line.

5   Darroch, Jacqueline E., Rachel K. Jones, and Stanley K. Henshaw. "Patterns in the Socioeconomic Characteristics of Women Obtaining Abortions in 2000-2001." *Perspectives on Sexual and Reproductive Health* 34(5). 2002. pp. 226-235. Web.

Seeking Peace from Minnesota to Mindanao

Anna Zaros

"Mining companies from your country, from the United States, come into our communities and degrade our cultural and societal norms through their labor practices, and through the consumerism they bring."

I was stunned into silence. What could I say to my Filipino friends as they vented their frustrations with my country?

"We have conflict in our communities because of the violence between the Moro Islamic Liberation Front and the government, and we also have conflict in our communities because we have to deal with these mining corporations degrading our culture and environment. It is unjust!"

I agreed. But how could I fix the situation as just one U.S. citizen interning in the Philippines?

"And to top it all off, the United States government has the government of the Philippines in Manila under its control. Our President Aquino will do anything to please the U.S. government, even if it means exploiting the resources of Mindanao and aggravating the ongoing armed conflicts that damage our society."

I scrambled for sympathetic words to reply.

I had arrived in the Philippines about a month and a half before for a six-month "field experience," a component of my graduate degree. I had been developing my conviction of the need for peace in our world for years, and this experience abroad was my chance to learn how to actually create peace in conflict-affected areas. I had dreamed of making a grand contribution to peace in the world. I wanted to be one of those amazing people who jet from country to country, mediate protracted conflicts, deliver humanitarian aid, spend the night schmoozing donors for more funds, and one day get nominated for the Nobel Peace Prize. Clearly, I had modest expectations. But now that I was in a real conflict setting in a foreign country, I was struggling to find my role.

I first became connected to issues of conflict and peace as an undergraduate. I started university as a passionate Catholic seeking to promote the Church and its social teachings. Through a number of social justice internships and theology classes, I felt increasingly drawn toward a focus on peace. As I learned more about conflicts like the ones in Darfur and Israel/Palestine, the need for peacebuilding in the world overwhelmed me.

Through these same classes and internships, I also learned of the wealth of resources for peace available within the Catholic Church. These resources included the tradition of Catholic social teaching, the example of the early Church's commitment to nonviolence, and the universal presence of the Church all over the world, working in various capacities for peace and justice. But I was disappointed to learn how underutilized these resources were. Daily, I wondered why so few people knew about the conflicts throughout the world. Why did campus ministry at my school focus so much on retreats and spirituality, and so little on social teaching? Why didn't more of my fellow Catholic students share my feelings of urgency about justice and peacebuilding?

Searching for answers to these questions led me to a yearlong volunteer program with the Sisters of St. Joseph of Carondelet in St. Paul, Minnesota. The Sisters were a rambunctious, graceful, and inspiring bunch. Most had dedicated themselves to decades of social justice work. I learned of Sister Rita Steinhagen, who founded a shelter for runaway youth. Later, she worked at a house of hospitality for undocumented immigrants fleeing violence and economic injustice in their countries. Sisters Kate and Ansgar Holmberg promoted justice through their art, and the McDonald sisters organized and participated in hundreds of nonviolent peace protests.

Jesus exemplified extreme inclusion, not only inviting into relationship those on the margins of society but also ministering to the people who were part of an oppressive system.

When I joined the Sisters for the yearly protest at the School of the Americas in Fort Benning, Georgia, I saw firsthand how their beliefs and spirituality brought both joy and serious dedication to the struggle for peace. At rest stops during the long drive to Georgia, the Sisters did the "Bunny Hop" around public restrooms, laughing as they shouted, "Close the SOA, close the SOA, hey, hey, hey!" Whereas I felt cranky and cramped from sitting for hours in a bus seat, the Sisters seemed to have limitless energy for peace in their sixtieth, seventieth, or eightieth years of life. Later, I watched these same Sisters lead a solemn funeral procession for those killed in conflict, offering up their sorrow over the violence and praying for healing for those affected—and for redemption for those committing atrocities.

The Sisters taught me that peacebuilding takes many forms. Their work ranged from addressing racial and class divides for peace within communities, to addressing domestic violence for peace within homes, to campaigning for an end to harmful U.S. foreign policy for peace within the world.

Their charism "to love God and dear neighbor without distinction" seemed a perfect motto for peacebuilding. I was inspired by how they followed Jesus' example from Scripture: a political activist who used nonviolent action to upend the establishment on behalf of the poor and oppressed. And he exemplified extreme inclusion, not only inviting into relationship those on the margins of society but also ministering to the people who were part of an oppressive system. Through my time with the Sisters, I was developing my own understanding of a Catholic theology of peacebuilding, one that was embedded in the principles of inclusion, unconditional forgiveness, and recognition of the divine in each person.

But was my ever-increasing passion enough? Would what I'd learned of Catholic peacebuilding apply to the world of civil wars, genocide, and torture? How could I translate my inspiration from Scripture and the lives of courageous religious leaders into practical peacebuilding around the world? To expand my understanding of peace, I went to graduate school for peace studies. After a year of coursework, my degree program sent me to Davao, a city in Mindanao, the conflict-affected group of islands in the Southern Philippines, for six months. Here, I would try to figure out how to apply all of my passion and education into building peace.

Tensions between Muslims (also called Moros in the Philippines), indigenous people (or Lumads), and Christians have existed in the Philippines since the Spanish attempted to conquer Mindanao from the sixteenth to nineteenth centuries. They never attained full control of Mindanao, but their efforts did embed deep-seated animosity in the relationship between the Moros and the Lumads who inhabited the island, and with the Christian colonizers.

When the Spanish sold the Philippines to the United States at the end of the nineteenth century, they included Mindanao, despite their lack of authority over this island group. Successive Philippine governments encouraged peasants from Luzon and Visayas, the other island groups of the Philippines, to migrate to Mindanao and take advantage of the "free land." Muslims and Lumads became minorities on their home island, lost ancestral lands, and became marginalized at the hands of a Christian government in the north.

As tensions escalated, both Christians and Muslims in Mindanao formed paramilitaries to protect their respective communities, and violence erupted. The Moro community ultimately united around the Moro National Liberation Front (MNLF), which fought for self-determination. Subsequently, as part of the institution of martial law in the Philippines in the early 1970s, dictator Ferdinand Marcos sent armed forces to Mindanao to squash the Moro forces. Violence escalated into civil war.

The MNLF and the government of the Philippines eventually signed a peace agreement in 1996, but some were dissatisfied with the agreement and upset over the failed promises of autonomy from Manila. The Moro Islamic Liberation Front (MILF), which had broken off from the MNLF years ago, continued fighting the government. Not only does violence continue today, but general mistrust, animosity, and prejudice among Muslims, Christians, and Lumads does as well, damaging the health of local communities.

For decades, peacebuilding activities have taken place all over Mindanao, including interreligious dialogues, local peace campaigns, political advocacy, and ceasefire monitoring. During my six-month internship, I researched Catholic peacebuilding in Mindanao with the aim of understanding who was doing Catholic peacebuilding, why they were doing it, and how their work could better contribute to the broader vision of peace in Mindanao. This is how I ended up at the Conference on Catholic Peacebuilding and Reconciliation, trying to figure out which peacebuilding tools, if any, I could employ to connect with these Mindanaoans so harmed by U.S. foreign policy and mining corporations in their communities.

The goal of the Catholic Peacebuilding and Reconciliation conference was to impress upon Catholics in Mindanao the importance of peace in the Catholic tradition. Since the major armed conflict in Mindanao is often marked by prejudice between Muslims and Christians, the majority of whom are Catholic, there is hope that harmony can prevail if more Catholics become peacebuilders. Catholics are the largest single religious group and hold many positions of power—so for peace to develop on this island, Catholics must be on board.

Most of the participants at the conference were Filipinos who work in local churches as priests, religious, or lay leaders. The key speakers were two American Catholic theologians, Robert Schreiter and Scott Appleby. The theologians presented their scholarship relating to reconciliation, peacebuilding, and the resources of the Catholic social justice tradition, while the Filipinos shared their experiences, successes, struggles, and ideas for living in and promoting peace amidst the conflict. I was surprised and inspired to learn from the presenters that rituals and sacraments, so familiar in Catholic communal life, are also important tools for peacebuilding. Rituals allow participants to share pieces of their worldview, giving others a glimpse of their beliefs and practices. This sharing can transform relationships into something new, something peaceful.

Eucharist is an important ritual that calls Catholics to embody such peacebuilding roles as presence and accompaniment. Eucharist can remind us to be present to people in conflict situations—just as Jesus is present to us in the breaking of bread that is his body—and to accompany those hurt by violence and even those who are the armed actors. Just as Jesus reached out to Pharisees, fishermen, and tax collectors, Catholic peacebuilders must reach out equally to amputees, widowed mothers, and guerilla fighters. By sharing in Mass together at the end of the conference, the participants enacted the importance of ritual and Eucharist. Many took the opportunity to state their commitment to peace and to the community shared at the conference. This felt deeply familiar, as it reminded me of the Sisters and their peace and justice work.

Eucharist can remind us to be present to people in conflict situations and to accompany those hurt by violence and even those who are the armed actors.

While the conference presenters delivered a powerfully optimistic message about the potential for Catholics to build peace, many community members at the conference expressed a lack of hope. The conference participants wanted to be peacebuilders, but they admitted, "We still don't know how." Many acknowledged their own prejudice against Muslims. Others saw the importance of interreligious dialogue and Catholic social teaching, but questioned whether these resources could address the political aspects of the conflict. And a few challenged whether there was a point in building peace in Mindanao at all when the United States had armed forces in the area, controlled the government in Manila, and continued to introduce conflict in the communities through its support of U.S.-based and international mining corporations.

Listening to the passion, despair, and pleas of the conference participants, I realized the paradoxical position I was in as I searched for a way to respond to the conflict. I was both insider and outsider. I was a Catholic, deeply believing in the importance of peacebuilding and the resources the

Catholic tradition offered for this work. I connected to the participants on this level. At the same time, I was an outsider, an American, a representative of a country responsible for some of the violence and oppression in the Philippines and in the lives of those sitting at the table with me.

This was a crucial test for me as a peacebuilder. How could I express genuine solidarity to these people whose communities were suffering? I fought the temptation to say, "I am only one citizen—what can I do?" Because I knew I bore some responsibility for the situation. Just as I am one of countless parts making up the Body of Christ, am I not also one part of a system of oppression?

I remembered the charism of the Sisters of St. Joseph of Carondelet, "to love God and dear neighbor without distinction." These Filipinos, who usually lived thousands of miles across the world from me, had always been my neighbors. So I listened to their stories; I agreed with their criticisms; I apologized and explained how corporations damage communities in the United States, too. I told an outspoken Sister about the Sisters of St. Joseph, assuring her that she had compatriots in the United States working tirelessly to change U.S. policy for the exact reasons she was citing.

Most importantly, I expressed my desire to learn as much about the Mindanao conflict as possible and to spread the stories of these peacebuilding pioneers in the United States. I would not let the voices of these courageous Mindanaoans go unheard.

I left Mindanao not sure if my presence there had made any difference. After being home for two months, I was asked to give a presentation on my experiences abroad to the students and faculty in my graduate program. This was my opportunity to tell the stories of my Filipino friends. I had the chance to reflect on the Catholic Church's rituals of forgiveness and healing and the Church documents promoting solidarity and justice. I explained how Catholic Filipinos called upon the example of Jesus in the Scriptures to prove the primacy of peacebuilding for Christians and how peacebuilders regularly participated in Mass to sustain themselves and their work. I spoke about the action steps to which the workshop participants committed themselves, such as attending more peacebuilding workshops, creating peace programs in their parishes, and reaching out to Muslims in their communities.

And I shared the uncertainty many of the Mindanoan Catholic peace-builders expressed. They believed in the importance of peace in their religious tradition and worked to incorporate Catholic teachings and practices into their work, but they were still honest in their struggle with their own prejudices toward Muslims, with a global oppressive system led by the United States, and even with fellow Catholics who saw no place for peace in their lives. In the Philippines, I learned that peace is a long and complicated process, full of setbacks and uncertainties. The role of Catholic peacebuilding within this process is still largely uncharted territory.

Nevertheless one thing stood out in the midst of the messiness: the deep human need for connection at the root of each conflict. Those in conflict need to feel reached out to, believed in, and heard. As the conference participants vented their frustrations, they were calling out in despair to anyone who could learn of their anguish and struggle to bring peace to their communities. In that moment, the best I could do for peace was to reach out to these participants, hear their cry for help, and respond in solidarity. Yes, I was an American, a part of the system of oppression, but I was also a sister in the human family and a fellow Catholic.

Solidarity, or companioning those who experience oppression, is a principle I first learned from Catholic social teaching and the example of Jesus. It is the main principle I follow in my quest to develop peace. But this drive to practice solidarity does not apply only within the realm of Catholicism; it also is a fundamental principle for practicing peacebuilding in any context.

I had connected with local Mindanaoans on the basis of our shared Catholic identity. While compassion, forgiveness, and presence are values taught in most religions or cultures, I learned them through my Catholic upbringing and education. The Catholic tradition, which, like other religious traditions, has been used to support violence, was being used to promote peace in the Philippines. What I had long searched for—Catholics living out the hard work of social justice and nonviolence in their lives—I found at last in Mindanao.

At the conference, we embodied Jesus' "Peace be with you" through our participation in the Eucharist. As I continue on my path as a peacebuilder, I picture Jesus sitting at tables listening to the suffering of those around him and empathizing as I hope I was able to do with my Filipino friends. Our Catholic rituals of embodiment give me the strength to genuinely say "I hear you," "I'm sorry," and "What can I do?"

Experiencing God in the Struggle to Define Myself

Phillip W. Clark

It takes something of great magnitude to move me to tears—November 4, 2008, was no exception. The television proclaimed that Illinois Senator Barack Obama had been elected as our nation's first African-American president. Historic significance notwithstanding, Barack Obama's victory carried with it a host of symbolic and meaningful implications for America. After enduring nearly a decade of political nihilism, obstructionism—some would even argue tyranny—at the hands of George W. Bush's administration, the American people had emerged into a new dawn, one brimming with the promises of hope and genuine change.

As much as people throughout the United States celebrated this, the promise of change resonated with me in a deeply personal way. Through my own tears of joy and accomplishment—this was the first election in which I was old enough to vote—a daring question resounded within me: "If such a momentous paradigm shift could be ushered in through the efforts of the American people, why couldn't the same happen within the Body of Christ?"

For most of my life, I knew that I was different from other boys. Since preschool, I noticed boys not simply as friends, but with a stronger intensity I could not yet define. As I grew older, I saw that this was not just curiosity or admiration; it was genuine attraction. When I came to terms with this, I was bewildered about what I should do next.

The taunting never drove me to despair, but it was a constant burden.

Although Catholic, during middle and high school I attended a private Christian academy affiliated with the Lutheran Church Missouri Synod. I had many happy memories there, and it is where I met most of my closest friends. But the environment of the school was very conservative and rigid. Nobody at the school was openly gay, and I wasn't ready to be the first. If anyone made an attempt to deviate from the school's cultural norm—whether in religion, politics, or even social exploits—others would regard them as "different" and "unusual."

I found this out the hard way. My very personality made me stand out. Most guys at the school were very athletic. I was not, so I circulated with the people with whom I had the most in common—who usually turned out to be girls. The other guys teased me about this. My friends were always by my side, so it never really seemed as if I was really being bullied. Yet in hindsight, when a certain group of people consistently and relentlessly ridicule and mock one individual, what other name is there for such behavior? The taunting, which singled me out for mannerisms perceived as different from most of the other guys in my class, never drove me to despair, but it was a constant burden. All of this became confounded when I found myself becoming attracted, inexplicably, to some of the same guys who ridiculed me.

Because my faith had always been an abiding and sustaining force in my life, I turned to it as I struggled through high school. As I investigated the pages of the Catholic Catechism, I was somewhat consoled and satisfied when I read, *"The number of men and women who have deep-seated homosexual tendencies is not negligible. They must be accepted with respect, compassion, and sensitivity. Every sign of unjust discrimination in their re-*

gard should be avoided. These persons are called to fulfill God's will in their lives and, if they are Christians, to unite to the sacrifice of the Lord's Cross the difficulties they may encounter from their condition."[6]

The fact that the Catechism described being homosexual as something a person did not intentionally or actively control comforted me. In many other expressions of Christianity, even identifying as a person attracted to the same sex could be construed as a sin. Growing up in a household headed by my mother, a single parent, I always wondered whether my father's absence contributed to my attraction to other men, as I'd heard so many outside parties insinuate. Yet, these feelings had always been present within me, only increasing in intensity as I grew older. I knew I had never made a decision to be attracted to boys—so it was a relief that the Catholic Church acknowledged this.

But my relief turned to dismay as I read on: *"This inclination, which is objectively disordered, constitutes for most of them a trial. Homosexual persons are called to chastity. By the virtues of self-mastery that teach them inner freedom, at times by the support of disinterested friendship, by prayer and sacramental grace, they can and should gradually and resolutely approach Christian perfection."*[7]

The Catechism added to my understanding of Bible-based arguments against homosexual relationships. My whole life, I had heard that God's most pivotal act of creation was making the human race. It was difficult for me to see the passages in Genesis where God creates humanity "male and female" and bids them to "be fruitful and multiply" in a different light. Even though I knew I had not chosen my feelings, I was not ready to accept sexual intercourse outside the context of a heterosexual marriage as good or moral. Biologically, at least, the evidence only seemed to confirm that human sexuality was divinely intended to be expressed within heterosexual matrimony.

Although I knew I was gay, I did not know why. Despite the constant presence of these feelings, I theorized that it made sense that expressing them could be wrong. After all, homosexual relations were flatly condemned in several instances throughout Scripture, weren't they? This last

---

6   *Catechism of the Catholic Church.* 2358.

7   *Catechism of the Catholic Church.* 2359.

point, more than anything else, resigned me to the life of chastity prescribed by the Catechism. I even saw such an existence as similar to a religious vocation that simply required me to relinquish expression of my sexuality for the sake of the Kingdom of Heaven. This inspired me, as I now saw my orientation as a vehicle to live out a higher calling destined to me by God. However, accepting this perceived calling did not prove an adequate "solution" to these feelings.

As I continued through high school, I watched most of my (straight) friends enter into committed and—at least for the time being—what appeared to me to be fulfilling relationships. Nevertheless, Christ's command, "Take up your cross, and follow Me," remained a constant refrain in my mind.

There was another refrain, uttered within the confines of the Sacrament of Reconciliation: "Bless me Father, for I have sinned...." Week after week, I appealed to God's mercy for the acts I committed in conflict with the Catechism's moral dictates. Any sexual activity outside marriage, even acts not involving other people, was morally prohibited. I must admit that I sustained this spiritual routine more out of fear of receiving the Eucharist in a state of mortal sin than of a genuine devotion to Confession. So great was my complex over maintaining my moral and spiritual purity that sometimes I went to immense lengths to participate in the Sacrament of Penance. On several occasions, I took a bus downtown to the Basilica of the Assumption, which had daily and extended hours for Confession—all so I could participate fully in the highlight of my week: the celebration of Sunday Eucharist. In hindsight, I wonder why I didn't ask myself sooner what I was really getting out of Holy Mass on Sundays if I just continued the same pattern of guilt, contrition, and despair.

After graduating, I found myself immersed in the outside world instead of the cultural cocoon my high school had been. I saw that people and society were not defined by the black and white ethical terms used to depict American culture in my religion classes. Most people were either indifferent to or completely accepting of those who were gay, lesbian, bisexual, or transgender—this was especially true of most others my age. This newfound feeling of acceptance, tolerance, and affirmation lead me to ponder anew how my innermost longings might be integrated with my Catholic faith.

Eventually, my curiosity got the best of me, and I began to investigate other theological points of view. Until then, I had simply accepted that the Church's hierarchy was divinely construed and not subject to challenge. But as I became familiar with the works of theologians and academics such as Hans Küng, Karl Rahner, Edward Schillebeeckx, John McNeill, Joan Chittister, and many others, I gravitated toward a new concept of the Church.

I came to understand the Church as an institution that developed within human history in the wake of the Resurrection under the auspices of the Holy Spirit. This was an ever-so-gradual process. The myth that Jesus had "ordained" twelve male apostles as the first priests to go forth and ordain subsequent priests and bishops no longer held any historical veracity for me.[8] As I began to see the Church as a very human undertaking, an ongoing adventure, a quest for God rather than a roadmap dropped from the hands of the ascending Christ, I reassessed many doctrines, viewpoints, and institutions in light of the cultural and historical climates in which they had originated, rather than as God's final word on a subject.

> **As I began to see the Church as a very human undertaking, an ongoing adventure, a quest for God, I reassessed many doctrines, viewpoints, and institutions.**

This was a profound light-bulb moment for my conscience. If the Catholic Church teaches that the creation account in Genesis does not have to be interpreted literally and that evolution is consistent with Church teaching, how far of a leap is it to suppose that the prohibitions against homosexuality are not meant to be taken literally either? Could these teachings be largely culturally constructed, rather than theologically and morally based?

As I contemplated these possibilities, I became more and more assured of who I was. Although I remained apprehensive about living my life as an openly gay man, I moved closer and closer to that reality with each passing day. And finally, as I took part in catapulting a man to the White House who never could have lived out such an aspiration half a century ago, the barriers

8   *Catechism of the Catholic Church.* 874.

of fear, resistance, and ignorance gave way within my heart.

The tears I shed that night were not only for a new era of hope within our nation, but also for a new era within my soul.

As I sought God in prayer in the wake of that happy revelation, a voice proclaimed within me, *"Fear not; I am with you; I made you as you are!"* A very public, political election had given way to a private, personal awakening. I left fear behind, stepping out of the isolation and uncertainty that had characterized most of my adolescence. And what I found was a life brimming with infinite possibilities.

Several months after embarking on this new path, I fell in love.

On a bright summer afternoon, I went to the LGBT community center in downtown Baltimore for a political meeting. As the evening progressed, a man sitting a few rows in front of me caught my attention. He had long hair pulled into a ponytail, a tall, athletic build, and captivating eyes. To me, he looked like the traditional depictions of Jesus Christ that adorn sanctuaries, churches, and the halls of art museums throughout the world. After the meeting, I worked up the courage to talk to him. By the end of the night, we had exchanged phone numbers.

Although this relationship was brief and filled with bouts of turmoil that ultimately would sever it, it provided me a window on what a blessing it could be to find love. I've never felt closer to the divine Source than when I enjoyed the romantic embrace of another man. The first sentences of Scripture encapsulate the intense feelings of warmth, joy, and love I felt in that moment: "...and the Spirit of God was hovering over the waters...."[9] God was tangibly present in that point in time, bestowing on me a benediction of assurance. Although that first relationship didn't last, I gained the conviction that the love my partner and I exchanged was not disordered or depraved but right and good. I was certain the very essence of the divine force we call "God," the very energy that animates and gives rise to all that can be temporally experienced, is Love.

It may be hard to discover hope in these dismal economic times. Despite the historic election of Barack Obama, very little of significance seems to have changed in our country's political landscape. Still, it remains imperative that we persevere in the face of the unknown and combat ignorance

9 Genesis 1:2

with a renewed vigor of reason, sincerely striving to comprehend the experiences of others with whom we may disagree. And we must share our own experiences so that all may be enriched to create a more perfect Union—within the United States, and within the Body of Christ. As I learned so well, we can only truly be free and fulfilled when we put our fears of the past behind us, embracing new and ever-changing points of reference that frame and shape what it means to be human beings who seek God.

Laying Injustice Down at the Feet of God

Erin Lorenz

I used to be a bit of a know-it-all regarding Catholicism. I was the good Catholic girl, the oldest of four children, with two younger brothers and a younger sister. As a teenager, I sang in the choir at Mass every Sunday and went to youth group every Thursday. I attended an all-girls Catholic high school, complete with plaid skirts. I have forty first cousins. I thought papal infallibility was silly but benign; I assumed women should be priests (and that it was just a matter of time before they would be—same with married clergy); and I believed that contraception, while maybe not the best idea ever, was certainly not the worst. Of course, abortion was evil. The death penalty was mostly evil. By the time I reached my senior year of high school, I defended all of these things to questioning classmates or non-practicing friends, and my contentment with Catholicism was teetering toward complacency.

All of it came apart the day after Easter, 2002. The child sex abuse scandal in Boston had been in the news for months. I had convinced myself of the standby excuses: people were witch-hunting or jumping on a bandwagon, the media was anti-Catholic. But then my parents sat us down for a family meeting and told us that a priest had abused Dad as a child. Dad, the master of carpentry and calculus homework, who had taught me to pray and to be an altar server, could barely look at us. I had never seen him so miserable. Everything I'd convinced myself of dissolved. Dad wasn't hunting for witches. He wasn't part of the anti-Catholic media. And all you had to do was look at him to see that if there had been any way to avoid having this discussion with us, he would have done it. This was no bandwagon. The scandal was real, and it was more brutal than even the media had made it sound.

Dad asked us not to tell anyone. Mom said she and my dad thought this issue had been addressed several years ago, which was the last time clergy sex abuse had been in the news. Seeing now that nothing had changed, they wanted to do something. They weren't sure what yet, but telling us was the first step.

I had no idea what to feel. I didn't want to think about it. So after the family meeting, we silently, uncomfortably went back to the rest of the evening. I called my aunt and uncle in Kentucky to confirm plans for the surprise anniversary party the four of us kids had been planning for our parents. I said nothing to Uncle John and Aunt Suzanne about what had just happened. They would be in town in July, they said, just in time for the party. They would love to come.

Not until I was settled into my first year at university did I finally figure out what to feel. I was watching an episode of *Without a Trace* that featured a pedophile. I felt weird, like I should be too upset to watch this. Except I did keep watching, and I was only as disturbed as anyone might be watching a show about a pedophile kidnapping a fourteen-year-old boy. It bothered me that I didn't feel more upset. Eventually, as Jack Malone began to ask the pedophile more and more explicit questions, I clicked off the TV.

I wanted to cry, just so I knew I felt something about what happened to Dad. But I didn't. I felt bad because I thought I should; and then I felt bad about that. The abuse didn't happen to me, did it? What business did I have feeling miserable or hurt or angry? The only thing I should feel was protective. As the oldest child, being protective came naturally to me. I decided to become very good at being protective.

From that point on, defending my family was my primary reason for participating in activities related to the clergy sex abuse issue. My parents' first real step into the reform arena was to establish a chapter of Voice of the Faithful. This was the product of about a year of research and prayerful discernment. My parents made it clear that they welcomed us at anything they organized or participated in, but that it was okay if we didn't go, too. This caused its own kind of tension. No one really knew how to talk about this to Dad, since we didn't want to bring up painful memories. So although we all would occasionally discuss new information or developments regarding the abuse issue, we didn't really talk about how we were all dealing with it. Participating in the Voice of the Faithful meetings was probably the best way we could all acknowledge our support for Mom and Dad. So I went. At a healing service, I sat with my mother so she wouldn't be alone while Dad spoke about and relived what had happened to him. I did this not because I thought I needed to heal. In fact, I thought I didn't. I just wanted to protect Dad.

I decided to become very good at being protective. But what was I protecting him from, really?

But what was I protecting him from, really? Maybe the outside world of doubters, those who claimed survivors were liars out for money, or from the bishops, who claimed that they hadn't known a thing about this (we promise!), or the papal loyalists who suddenly found schisms and heresies in every questioning of authority. The witch-hunt, it could be said, now went both ways. I had to protect my family from being burned at the stake. But when corrupt Church leaders want someone to burn, they have far more resources at their disposal than an eighteen-year-old girl does.

This became abundantly clear in 2006, when legislation in Annapolis attempted to increase the statute of limitations to the age of forty-two for civil cases of child sexual abuse. As it was, if an abuse survivor did not press charges before he or she turned twenty-five, the abuser could not be brought to trial. Now a senior in college, I drove down to the State House to explain that my father hadn't told us, his own children, about the abuse until well into his forties. I didn't testify for my own sake—but I wasn't letting my parents go it alone.

The state legislature played right into the hands of the diocesan lobbyists. They postponed the testimony on our bill in an attempt to get our witnesses to leave. The worst part was, I did leave—I had to get back to class. When it became obvious that I would not be able to speak, I stalked out of the assembly room and cried. I'd tried to protect my family, to get up and talk for ninety seconds, and they—the lawyers and the lobbyists and the lawmakers and the clergy—kept me from doing this one thing.

My protectiveness transformed into anger—anger that often turned to frustration because I felt like there was so little I could do. With Voice of the Faithful, my parents were trying to gain support for survivors and find ways to keep the clergy accountable, but I was frustrated and angry about the lack of progress. This anger simmered slowly over the next four years, sometimes boiling over in a rant to a friend or a post in my online journal. I did a lot of reading during that time—Thomas Cahill, Richard McBrien, Joan Chittister, Gary Wills, Joyce Rupp, and the lone conservative, Christopher West. I tried to read a few other conservative thinkers, but they all seemed to blindly trust the Church authorities, and I no longer could.

It may seem odd to be excited when news of clergy sex abuse pours into the mainstream media, but that's how I felt when Europe went up in flames over the scandal during Lent, 2010. Now the world would know what my family had known for years: that the Church was septic with this infection. Now, with the facts public and on our side, we—not just my family, but also all survivors and anyone who supported them—could fight it.

So on Good Friday, Voice of the Faithful organized a vigil/Stations of the Cross/press conference across the street from the National Cathedral in Washington, D.C. My whole family was there, including my brother's very pregnant wife.

It was a beautiful day, but the air was heavy. Time moved like molten lead. As we prayed through the Stations, I caught sight of Cardinal Wuerl's fuchsia robe. He just stood there, piously working through the Stations. I could find no good reason for him to be there. He had met with my parents earlier during his tenure as the Archbishop of Washington, but he had told my father to seek healing and come back when he had made peace with the Church. He had made it clear that he had no interest in listening to suggestions from anyone who had actually survived the trauma he claimed he was trying to prevent. After the liturgy, Wuerl found my father. I hung on my brother's arm to keep from throwing myself in front of Dad and telling Wuerl and anyone else in a Roman collar to step off.

I realized then that my hurt wasn't just for my father— it was for me, too.

How many times had Church leaders said stupid and insensitive things about child abuse? That it was in the past, that the survivors needed to reconcile with the Church (as if the survivors were the ones who needed to seek forgiveness), or that their non-binding guidelines were sufficient to prevent further abuse and cover-ups. No compassion, no listening…just talking points that, according to many survivors, were entirely unhelpful if not painful to hear. The bishops' ignorance and uncaring had hurt Dad again and again. And yet there Dad was, talking to Wuerl about what had happened to him, hurting again—and for what? As far as I could tell, it was just so Wuerl could look as if he was involved with the victims when the cameras pointed at him. Cardinal Wuerl said polite things to Dad that day. But nothing in the Archdiocese of Washington changed to protect more kids or support more survivors.

After the vigil, I went home and sat on the couch, grateful to be alone. I didn't really want to watch our vigil on the news—I felt bled out. I didn't move for a long time, except to work the remote. We had made the evening news on several stations.

It slowly occurred to me that I still had to go to Good Friday service at our parish. The thought made me want to cry from exhaustion. So I didn't go. It was the first and only time I consciously chose not to attend an important liturgy because of the abuse.

I had already observed Good Friday by my presence at the vigil, and I didn't want to go again—because I hurt. For the first time, the abuse was my pain, too. Like the Church, a family is one body, and when one member hurts, so do the others. I realized then that my hurt wasn't just for my father—it was for me, too. The past eight years had destroyed my trust in Church authority. I had once defended Church leaders to my friends, even when they thought I was going too far. I had given the bishops and the popes the benefit of the doubt, read their literature, formed my conscience around their teachings, confessed to them my sins, called them by their titles, all while they were peddling children to the devil. They had shamed the community that Jesus had begun so many centuries ago, and they had exposed my God, the One they convinced me to love and trust, to the insults of the world. So on Good Friday, I allowed myself to suffer and hurt, maybe a bit like the women at the foot of the cross. Then I mourned the betrayal, and my Church, which, for all I could see, was crumbling away.

If Renée, fully aware of the problems in this Church, could freely join herself to it, and if we were happy about that, then somehow things would be okay.

The following night, at the Vigil Mass, eight Easters after that awful family meeting, we welcomed my sister-in-law, Renée, into the Catholic Church. We wondered when we would welcome the baby she was carrying into the world. Just one day after the protest, we were celebrating Renée's First Communion and Confirmation. Even Dad was smiling, watching her up on the altar, angling himself and his camera to get a good shot.

This happiness was significant. If Renée, fully aware of the problems in this Church, could freely join herself to it, and if we were happy about that, then somehow things would be okay. The words Jesus spoke to St. Peter about the Church came rushing into my head: "The gates of hell shall not prevail against it." I believed him.

Eager to prevail against the hell we'd witnessed, my parents and I found ourselves at a Survivor's Voice gathering in Rome—not without trepidation—on October 31, the anniversary of Martin Luther's famous trip to the Wittenberg Cathedral. We didn't know who or how many would show up, or if it would have any impact. We planned to hold a candlelight vigil and present survivors' letters and stories to whichever Church official would open the door. However, the ever-sensitive Vatican personnel prohibited us from gathering at our intended location—St. Peter's Square—and so we gathered five hundred meters away instead. We were still well within sight of St. Peter's.

A line of low-level Italian military officers kept us from crossing the street to enter the piazza. A few organizers received a police escort into the square to lay rocks down as a temporary memorial to victims and survivors. I wanted to go into the piazza, too, so I fell in with a group of tourists and waited to cross the street. I looked up at the guard as the light changed, wondering if he would challenge me. He looked away, and I crossed the street without incident.

I expected to feel anger as I approached the church. Here it was, this symbol of corruption, perversion, and fear. With each step, St. Peter's grew a little bigger. But instead of being imposing and forbidding, the gargantuan church seemed friendly, all lit up in its squareness, nestled at the head of the piazza. It reminded me of a big La-Z-Boy recliner, where your grandpa might sit by the fire and tell stories. My anxiety fell behind me as I picked up speed, marching right up to the gate separating the square from the church steps. I stood there for a moment. St. Peter materialized in my imagination.

"You know," he said, "I didn't tell them not to let you in."

"I know." I continued gazing up at the basilica.

"They don't live here, remember. They live behind the church. Over to your right."

I looked in the general direction of the other Vatican buildings. "Yeah."

Pause.

"I didn't mean for any of this to happen," he said.

"I know."

"It is good that you are here."

"Thanks."

Pause.

"Do you think this will ever get better?" I asked.

"Yes."

"How?"

Silence. St. Peter dissolved back into my subconscious. Some might call that prayer, or simply self-comfort. I can live with either. But I think St. Peter remained silent on my last question because I was already living the answer: I was laying my fight down.

Peter the Rock could bear the weight of this crisis, and the God who made all things could transform it. Maybe God was asking me to lay it down: "You do not need to protect them anymore. Remember, I make all things new. Lay it here, keep laying it here, where it belongs! I will make it new."

I do not know how God will make this Church new, but I no longer see futility. Instead, I have hope. The current structure of celibate men deciding how the Church will function simply will not last. For too long this institution has harbored too many secrets and lies that ought to have seen the light decades ago—without the aid of subpoenas or police raids. Breaking down such a corrupt structure is essential to the protection of children, as well as to the Church's survival as a positive and relevant presence in the world. Martin Luther King, Jr., wrote that time is neutral and will not change things simply by its passing. Instead of waiting for crucial changes—married clergy, women's ordination, and the transparency that will keep children safe—to happen, I need to help make it happen. How to do this is not always clear, but it is less of a fight for me now, and more of a welcome challenge. All I can do is lay the injustice down at the feet of God and those responsible, and then I let the Holy Spirit do the rest. For now, that is enough.

Justice in a Hospital Room

Lauren Ivory

As my high school Spanish teacher told me my mom needed to talk to me in the hallway, she tried to sound casual. But I knew this would not be a short conversation, because the teacher was also packing my books away. The strained look on my mom's face confirmed that something was wrong.

"Grandpa is sick," she said. "We need to go to Detroit."

I didn't ask her anything as we walked to the car, afraid to learn what I did not want to hear. Back home, I tried to will my grandpa well by refusing to pack anything black—I wasn't going to Detroit for a funeral.

Mom and I didn't get seats together on the plane. We didn't even have the presence of mind to ask someone to switch with us. Instead, my mom sat behind me and we held hands between the seats and cried while taking off.

My grandfather had suffered a brain aneurysm, which would take his life. At the hospital, a chaplain approached my family. She was a small woman, maybe five feet tall, but she was about to have a huge impact on me. In some sort of unspoken communication, my whole family—Mom, sisters, Grandma, aunts, and uncles—ushered her over to me. Maybe it was because I was crying so much, or because I had a budding interest in spirituality. Whatever the reason, they seemed relieved that she was there.

Despite my grief, I was very taken with the chaplain—being Catholic, I had never met a female minister before. I wiped away the tears and asked her, "What do you do?"

She told me that she came to be with people when they were struggling and tried to help if she could. I thought, *They pay you just to be nice to people? I want that job!* (Now that I, too, work as a hospital chaplain, I know that there is much more to this work than being nice. I have come to believe that accompanying people on their spiritual journeys is an important part of creating a more just world.)

My journey from that hospital room to chaplaincy was not a straight path. When I went to college, I had a vague notion that I would look into this chaplaincy thing. Then I took a theology class "for fun" at my Catholic college and fell in love. Studying theology locked into my passion for ideas like God's love for all people, human dignity, stewardship of the environment, and respect for all creation.

As I met other Catholics who worked to realize these values in the world, I thought, *Surely, this is where I am meant to be. This is what's important.* I worked in the social justice office in campus ministry. I planned events and speakers and went to protests. I even got arrested for civil disobedience at a vigil demanding the closure of the U.S.-funded School of the Americas (now called WHINSEC), a combat training school for Latin and South American soldiers whose graduates have committed some of the worst crimes against humanity in history.

I thought that if I was willing to get arrested then I must be doing what I was meant to do. I continued to learn about one heartbreaking reality after another: the violation of workers' rights and safety in sweatshops and migrant farming, the suffering of sex trade workers in the U.S. and abroad, the effects of over-consumption on the natural resources others need simply to survive. Where else would God have me spend my energy when suffering like this was going on?

But after finishing graduate school and working as a campus minister for justice initiatives, I found myself worn out, depressed, and disheartened. Why wasn't I clicking with this kind of work? Why did it feel forced? I didn't understand how I could dread work so much when I was doing things I thought were of the utmost importance. I couldn't understand why I had to struggle to motivate people to get involved, especially because I was so passionate about justice. I began to feel disconnected from the people I felt most concerned about—namely, those suffering from homelessness, illness, and violence. Instead of organizing others to help homeless people, I wanted to be out there helping homeless people. Activism was not life giving for me, but at the time I thought it was the most important thing a Christian could do.

Where else would God have me spend my energy when suffering like this was going on?

I finally decided to enter chaplaincy full time after doing part-time on-call and overnight shifts in graduate school. As a chaplain resident, I found the life-giving work I craved. It was the first job I'd ever had where I truly understood the concept of relying on God's grace. When people told me I'd played an important role in helping them through their suffering, I had no idea how I had done it—and I couldn't comprehend how I could see all of this suffering and not be depressed by it myself. On the flip side, I came away from chaplaincy work with energy. After my experience doing social justice ministry and feeling woefully inadequate, I thoroughly enjoyed feeling so in sync with my work.

My love affair with the word *exactly* began at this time. I often "sum up" what a person has been telling me or ask a question to clarify whether I understand. When the patient or family member responds, "Exactly," I know I've done my job well.

I don't do chaplaincy work for the praise or acclamation. I do it because I know how transformative good listening can be. I had spent my life tending to the pain of others while ignoring my own. My family struggled with a terrible divorce, the pain enduring long after the papers were signed. Somewhere along the line, I became the family peacemaker. I hated to see people fight, and because people talked to me when they wouldn't talk to one another, I saw their misconceptions and misunderstandings getting in the way of a harmonious home—the thing I wanted most of all. It was a daunting job, especially for an eleven-year-old, but I learned the role well and kept it up for many years. Not surprisingly, I became a resident assistant in college so I could keep helping people. Luckily, I also took advantage of a "suggestion" by our supervisor that each of us see a school counselor at least once every semester. I finally had the impetus to seek help for myself: By doing so, I reasoned, I could better help others.

Clinical pastoral education came just in time. The training program for hospital chaplains teaches that you have to look at your own issues; if you hide from them, they might affect the ones you care for by coming out in subconscious ways. At first I did the hard work because it would make me a better chaplain. But then I kept having experiences that told me God was sneaking in some help just for me. Interacting with a patient's family would give me insight into my own family. Sometimes even reflecting on the deaths I witnessed brought me life-giving awareness. God was bringing healing and insight into my life through the reflections I hoped would help me grow for the sake of others.

I began to wonder why I constantly found courage to advocate for and protect others, but not myself. I remember attending a haunted house once and being scared off my rocker. But when one of the youngest kids panicked, I jumped into action, shielding her from the ghouls and goblins around us. No one was more surprised than me by my actions; given my own fears, I know I tapped into a deeper source of courage in that moment.

In a similar way, offering pastoral care gave me strength I had not had before. I began to realize that my fight for others was really a fight for myself. I struggled toward believing that God's love for all included me. I no longer felt guilty that I wasn't doing "justice work." I realized that helping people see their own self-worth is a form of justice work. Societal systems or loved ones who tell people they are not worth fair, safe, or humane treatment do immense psychological and spiritual harm. Often, my patients are case studies of the global atrocities of injustice many only encounter in the news.

Take, for instance, the twenty-four-year-old man I met who suffered multiple-organ failure due to unsafe working conditions. He was an undocumented immigrant whose bosses didn't comply with worker safety laws because they knew their employees wouldn't report the conditions. A black man I worked with at a different hospital told me about the racism he encountered almost daily. Patients and families would assume he was an assistant in his department instead of the director; the look of surprise on their faces when they heard the truth felt shaming to him. Humbled by his trust in me, I simply apologized—not on behalf of our coworkers but as a person who acknowledged the hurt he suffered. He began to cry and explained that his tears were of relief—finally, someone had acknowledged what he experienced so often.

> **I realized that refusing people the space to grieve was a form of injustice.**

Around this time, I realized that refusing people the space to grieve was a form of injustice as well. All too often we minimize people's suffering because we feel uncomfortable; we don't mean harm, but we are naturally oriented away from negative feelings and want to avoid other people's sadness. I also saw for the first time how our religious beliefs can work against our own sense of self-worth and our ability to process grief.

For example, I met a woman who told me about a rape she endured years before. She said, "I know people say everything happens for a reason, but I just can't see how in this situation." As she tried to reconcile the trauma of rape with her faith in a loving God, she kept telling herself that she must have "deserved" the rape or that it would at least result in some good in the end. This perspective kept her distant from God, whom she resented for "giving" her such a painful experience. Hesitantly, I told the woman that not everyone believes everything happens for a reason; would she like to talk about some of the other ways people view this issue? Her eyes lit up and she agreed. As we talked, she found a way to address the injustice of her rape, as well as the injustice of the religious worldview she accepted—but could never make sense of—in the midst of her suffering.

Some might be cynical about the ability to effect change in individuals, or they might question the worthiness of concentrating on one person's life when there are "bigger fish to fry." Others might ask what difference it makes to help one person when so many injustices stem from problems at the national or global level. I don't know what happens when my patients go home, but I often see change happening for people when we talk, and that's enough for me. I am proud of moments when I can defend the dignity of a person who gets overlooked: talking to the staff person who doesn't want to call a transgendered patient by her preferred name just because her driver's license says she is male; tending to a man's grief when his live-in girlfriend was badly hurt in a car accident; or even explaining to a staff member why I admire a certain belief from a religious group that is often marginalized.

Although I moved away from it as I discerned my calling to chaplaincy, social justice activism did help me understand how God was calling me to act for justice. Through God's ironic sense of humor, as I began to stand up for others' rights I started to honor my own and embrace my own dignity. No longer did I see myself as important only if I were helping someone else; I could spend energy on me just for me. It's as though God saw what I was doing and thought, "Hey, maybe this could be an inroad to convince her of her own goodness."

Activism convinced me that I, like the people whose rights I fought for, am worthy of fair treatment, love, and concern. When I went to the protest where I got arrested for "trespassing," I thought I was standing up for others' rights. Yet it was also a concrete act that helped me grow more sure of my own rights, not the least of which was to stand up for what I believed.

I call the work I do now "interpersonal justice." I try to establish and maintain a just culture in my work environment: supporting coworkers, calling attention to unjust actions or practices, and encouraging people to heed their convictions. But my work affects justice within individuals as well, and I enjoy theorizing about how this justice work on a personal level can affect justice at the community and global levels. When people heal, it's bound to affect their relationships and the way they interact in the world. Lives can change, relationships can change, deadbolts can be unlocked; a person can finally find healing, move forward from grief, and even experience a corresponding improvement in physical health.

As a chaplain, I can give a man a safe space in which he can express the deep fear and pressure he feels being the main breadwinner for his family in a terrible economy. I can help a woman find relief by filling out an advanced directive for medical care so her life partner can legally make decisions for her. I can tell people they are important by giving them quality time and quality listening. I am very privileged to witness these graced moments and humbled that God would partner with me to facilitate them.

The people I meet every day represent the face of suffering, yes, but they also show me the face of healing and restoration. They show me resurrection in very tangible and inspiring ways. Frederick Buechner wrote, "The place God calls you to is the place where your deep gladness and the world's deep hunger meet."

I feel fortunate to have found that place.

Remaining Faithful in a Flawed System

José L. Martinez

More often than not when you grow up Catholic, routine becomes the name of the game.

My family is thoroughly Catholic. We went to Mass every Sunday at 10:00 a.m. (or at 5:30 p.m. when we didn't wake up on time). We muttered under our collective breath on Christmas and Easter because the heavy influx of churchgoers made finding a spot in the parking lot a true exercise of faith. When I got confirmed, I chose the name *Marco* because I figured people would laugh less when the bishop said it aloud than if I'd chosen the name I actually wanted, *Ignacio*. (To say I was a self-conscious kid would be a gross understatement.) My family passed through phases of zeal, vowing to sit down every night and pray together, a routine that usually lasted only a couple weeks at a time.

I knew the words, I knew the moves, I knew when to sit and stand and kneel. I even knew some of the ins and outs of the theology, which earned me straight A's in religion classes throughout elementary and high school—although, to be fair, it was easy to get an A in religion class. (Knowing what teachers were looking for on questions like "Is God love?" didn't really fuel any all-nighters for me.) But despite all that, religion was just something I did, and something that could get me in trouble if I didn't do it right. I didn't really think about who would get me in trouble. I never viewed God as the punishing type, so the likeliest candidate was the austere priest from my parish with a really thick Spanish accent who would sporadically yell during his hard-to-decipher homilies.

Then, one Sunday evening as I was packing away the drum set I played at youth Mass, Jason and Crystalina Evert—a well-known couple who travel the country speaking to teenagers about chastity—approached me. They told me that in their prayer before Mass, they felt affirmed that I should be on their talk show on the Eternal Word Television Network (EWTN), where teens and young adults from across the country discussed chastity. Since I'd never met either of them, I was slightly weirded out, and definitely not as smooth as I like to think I am in situations in which I'm surprised with an offer of a TV role.

Not realizing that I still wouldn't be famous after the show, I eagerly agreed to fly out to EWTN's studios in Birmingham, Alabama, for a spot on *The Pure Life*.

I'm glad I did. When I met the other teens filming the series, it was pretty clear why each of them were there. Two of them were already on the chastity speaking circuit. Some were committed pro-life activists. Almost all could spout theological doctrine as if it were pop culture trivia. And then there was me: the kid from San Diego who didn't get that upset about missing Mass sometimes and didn't know much of anything about the late Pope John Paul II, and even less about the latest encyclical. (I also had to look up what an encyclical was, mostly because everyone kept referring to the wisdom of the most recent one that they'd apparently read for pleasure.) But for the first time, I was excited about being Catholic, because I saw how excited my fellow (young) cast members were about it. So I learned how to be Catholic in their by-the-book, completely-in-line-with-everything-the-magisterium-says way.

After two weeks of filming the thirteen-episode series, I returned from Alabama and became what I thought was the prototypical orthodox Catholic teenager. I picked up books on theology from the library and made sure they had official Church approval before I read them. I went to praise and worship concerts as often as I could. I carried a Rosary in my pocket, which I "accidentally" withdrew along with my keys or phone sometimes, just so others knew how pious I was. And while I did have some genuine faith experiences during this time, a lot of it was a façade. Take the Eucharistic procession at a Steubenville San Diego conference: I really did have a powerful experience kneeling in front of the priest as he walked by and, at that moment, I felt as if I were following Jesus in his ministry in Galilee two millennia before. But the tears I cried were forced—because everyone around me was falling to the ground weeping. I was doing what I thought that group back in Alabama would approve of.

To me, those kids in Alabama represented Catholicism done right. Their knowledge of the minutiae of our faith that nobody seemed to know—did you know that the altar server who swings the censer (which I previously referred to as "the thing you swing the incense from") is called the thurifer?—was so attractive to me that I wanted them to accept me. Perhaps then, I thought, I'd find that sense of belonging I longed for. Among the cast of *The Pure Life* I'd caught a glimpse of what it might be like to belong to a world Catholicism—an international faith, shared by millions of human beings. That's really attractive to a teenager who's about to attend college, where the student with no identity is among the lonely ones. All I had to do to be accepted was make myself acceptable through my beliefs, practices, and rhetoric. So I did.

And because I did, I entered college with a lot of ideas I thought were done developing. The magisterium's authority was definitive and final and not to be challenged. Roman Catholicism held the fullness of truth. Abortion was a non-negotiable issue. Living chastely was a black-and-white decision with no room for discussion. Gender could and should define roles in the Catholic Church. These were my positions as I began my theology major at Loyola Marymount University in Los Angeles, a course of study that my orthodox friends had warned me against. "Those Jesuits do bad theology!" they said. If by "bad theology" they meant that LMU would force me to rethink everything I knew about theology, God, and being Catholic and start from scratch by critically constructing a more personally challenging and fulfilling theology—then they were absolutely right.

In my theology classes, the professors asked the "what-if" questions I'd been trained to think were wrong. I held class discussions with people who weren't practicing Catholics, who weren't Catholic at all, who didn't even believe in God. A close friend of mine who works on LMU's staff still laughs when he recalls the first time I went to him in confidence and told him, "One of my theology professors isn't Catholic. Is that weird?" I'd been a cradle Catholic who'd remained largely unexposed to the world beyond suburban Catholicism, and then I'd become an active Catholic who only surrounded myself with like-minded people. It's really hard to do that in college.

The professors asked the "what-if" questions I'd been trained to think were wrong.

For a while, I still acted with the Alabama crew in mind, even as more and more people around me critically engaged their faith and religion. Two pivotal events during my sophomore year, one on the heels of the other, changed that. First, I wrote an opinion article for LMU's student newspaper about why I was voting for the pro-choice Barack Obama. I focused on the perils of voting based on a single issue—in this case, abortion—but from the angry responses I received I might as well have condoned abortion as an acceptable method of population control. The responses personally attacked me, and I really struggled through the post-publication phase. But after all was said and done, I hadn't died or anything. In fact, I'd survived an exhausting process. I had come to the conclusion that, politically, Obama was the best candidate. When I weighed that against my faith, I realized that I believed Obama's views on other social justice issues were as important, if not more important, to me than the single issue of abortion. And I didn't believe that taking this position, after deep reflection, was incompatible with being a good Catholic—even in the face of heavy condemnation by most of the orthodox Catholics I knew.

Shortly afterward, I went to Fort Benning, Georgia, with a group from LMU for the annual protest against the School of the Americas (SOA), officially known as the Western Hemisphere Institute for Security Cooperation (WHINSEC). The organizer of this protest, Maryknoll priest Roy Bourgeois, has drawn ire from both the Vatican and orthodox Catholics because of his position on a justice issue unrelated to WHINSEC: Father Roy publicly supports women's ordination. When one of LMU's campus ministers mentioned this to me, I knew that all Father Roy's efforts to promote justice would be tainted by this heretical belief. It was hard for me to see him as a "true" Catholic—I wasn't about to say women could be priests (tradition), even if I was voting for Barack Obama. But the journalist in me beat out the tradition-happy Catholic when my editor at the school newspaper asked me to interview Father Roy at the protest.

In talking to the priest, I saw that his conviction—that barring women from the priesthood is unjust and unloving—was real. His pain on behalf of women who felt excluded from the Catholic Church was real. The Vatican had recently threatened to excommunicate him if he didn't recant, and the pain of being punished for remaining true to his conscience was eating away at him. As he explained this to me, his voice was pained—pleading, almost.

"I think sometimes, especially we as clergy and also as people of faith, become very selective about justice issues," he said. "Having been a priest for thirty-six years, I simply cannot in conscience be silent about injustice in my Church. The exclusion of women from the priesthood is a grave injustice. Sexism, like racism, is a sin." He wouldn't recant, he told me, and he told Rome the same thing. Then he met with his family, who threw their support behind him. "I wept," he said. "And I felt such peace of mind."

Then he asked me if I'd like to meet a woman priest.

Again, a fierce internal struggle between José the Journalist and José the Catholic. Would I get in trouble if I were seen with a woman claiming to be a priest? But I still needed to fill my word count, so I said yes. That's how I met Janice Sevre-Duszynska, the thirty-fifth woman ordained by the activist group Roman Catholic Womenpriests. To my surprise, I liked her. She wore a colorful, flowing shawl and had kind eyes. Her face was poised with determination. I was so struck by her humility; she insisted that I call her "Janice," without any titles, wanting me to understand that she and I were on the same level—something I'd never really seen a priest do. I also couldn't help but admire her conviction, despite the brutal backlash—like when one attendee at the WHINSEC protest laughingly referred to her as a "crazy, heretical bitch." In contrast, I'd almost forgotten I was supposed to think she was a heretic.

As much as I fought it, Janice had given me an image to carry with me on my journey to define my own faith, an image that would constantly remind me that God's voice and work isn't limited to the voice and work of the magisterium: the image of a strong, faithful woman wearing priestly garb.

I started writing more progressive columns. Most people were thrilled to see me engaging questions of faith, especially my mentors on LMU's Campus Ministry staff and my theology professors. Some were upset, like an LMU student's parent who sent me an all-caps email calling my writing "CRUDE" and claiming that I didn't fully understand the depth of my "LOVING RESPONSIBILITY" as a Catholic writer to be obedient. My own parents, who'd grown up Catholic in the same way I did, started asking questions, too, emailing their theology-major son to help clarify their own thinking.

I used my studies to tackle these questions. For a theological ethics course, I wrote a paper on why the Catholic Church was morally obligated to restore women's eligibility to be ordained.[10] By the middle of my senior year, I'd decided that the Catholic Church was sexist in ways that went against its message of inclusive love. If the Church says the first shall be last and the last shall be first, why do its laws, doctrine, and rules for proper practice of faith create more marginalized and disenfranchised people? The marginalized people I felt drawn to were women. This is what I wrote my 78-page thesis on. But, as many of my friends were kind enough to point out, I'm not a woman. (Glad they noticed.) So why had this question grasped me so tightly? Why did it matter so much?

It mattered because I'd learned about the power of experience. My ethics courses identified four main sources for ethical development: Scripture, tradition, experience, and dialogue. The Catholic Church privileges Scripture and tradition, viewing human experience—what people actually go through—in light of those. But what happens when destructive attitudes

10 The language of restoration refers to historical evidence that indicates that in early Christian communities, women were indeed recognized as ordained. As the institutional Church grew, however, so did sexist sentiment; eventually, women were disallowed from serving in the capacity of ordained ministry. To learn more, see Gary Lacy's *The Hidden History of Women's Ordination*.

about women appear in Scripture and tradition? I gravitated toward experience as the source of my ethics. The experience of meeting the group from *The Pure Life* had triggered this entire journey; the experience of meeting Father Roy and Janice deepened my understanding of what it means to be faithful. Experience had revealed truth to me, and now I was becoming more strongly convinced that it was a crucial part of figuring out how the Catholic Church could better love and justly treat all its members, whether women or men.

That same Catholicism was telling half its members that they could only belong in a limited way because of their sex.

My experience has privileged me to be surrounded by strong, faithful women and men whose lives are examples of the love and gentleness and firm conviction that Jesus exemplified—whether they do it in Jesus' name or not.

I've listened to close female friends tell me that they'd love to be priests and to female mentors who have the same administrative and pastoral skills as those in ordained leadership. But they know they can't receive that same ordination—unless they want to be vilified like Janice.

The reluctant tears and clenched fists and sighs of resignation that accent these stories remind me how real the women's struggle is inside the Catholic Church. These stories become all the more poignant when I remember that the reason I latched on to Catholicism in the first place was because I wanted to belong somewhere. And now that same Catholicism was telling half its members that they could only belong in a limited way because of their sex.

I see this as a huge problem within the tradition I call home. But I continue to call it home, because Church is about belonging. I belong to a community of believers that call themselves Catholic. But now, instead of being the appeaser—the guy who carried a Rosary around even though he never prayed one, or the guy who proclaimed total obedience to the pope even though he hadn't really thought it through—I've come to a fuller awareness of what it means to be Catholic.

Just like I can never leave my family, I don't think I can leave Catholicism. It's part of who I am. But just like I'd challenge my family members out of love if I saw them doing wrong, I will challenge my Church when I see it not fully living up to its identity. And while *The Pure Life* group may be horrified that I no longer buy into every official belief, or even into the definition of chastity they taught me, I'd like to talk to them about it, because now I can actually defend my views on what responsible sexuality is.

Because while there's no flawless religious tradition, it doesn't mean I can't work toward something better. Fitting in and belonging was simply the first step; now I have to act on the faith I've found. For now, that means being what some disparagingly call a "cafeteria Catholic": only following certain aspects of the tradition and willfully not following others. Some might think this is lazy, but I consider it a moral obligation. I'm working to live out a faith that's both meaningful to me and true to its own message of inclusive love. This means I have to go beyond just listening to stories and tell my own: why I choose to be a Catholic in this way, and why I think Catholics need a better roadmap than the one the magisterium currently provides.

As we work toward that, we wait in joyful hope.

About the Editors

Lacey Louwagie is a librarian and freelance writer and editor with a degree in English from the College of St. Benedict in St. Joseph, Minnesota. Lacey was raised on a farm in rural Minnesota, near the town of Cottonwood, and now lives in a cozy little house in South Dakota with her husband, Ivan VenOsdel, and their cats and dog.

Kate Ward is a Ph.D. student in theological ethics at Boston College. She earned an A.B. from Harvard in psychology and an M.Div. from Catholic Theological Union. Originally from Albany, NY, she lives in Boston with her husband, the talk show host Matthew Filipowicz.

Together they edit www.youngadultcatholics-blog.com, a blog for young adult catholics.

About the Contributors

Phillip W. Clark is a pre-law student in Baltimore, Maryland, where he was born and raised.

Magalí Cecilia Del Bueno was born in Buenos Aires and raised in Southern California and now lives in Lomita, California, where she is a religion and social studies teacher for sixth, seventh, and eighth grades at a Catholic school. She also volunteers with the non-profit organization Build a Miracle.

Johanna Hatch, originally from the East Coast and currently living with her family in Verona, Wisconsin, is a doula and childbirth educator, as well as a full-time student.

Lauren Ivory, originally from Iron River, Michigan, now resides in Chicago, Illinois, where she works as a hospital chaplain.

Erin Lorenz was born and raised and currently resides in Bowie, Maryland, where she teaches English by day and directs school plays by night.

José L. Martinez, a San Diego native currently living in Los Angeles, California, is a reporter for a radio station, working the South L.A. beat.

Bill Przylucki, originally from Albany, New York, is presently a community organizer in Los Angeles, California.

Katherine Schmidt from Yorktown, Virginia, is currently a doctoral student in Dayton, Ohio.

Justin Sengstock from Chicago Heights, Illinois, and currently living in Steger, Illinois, is a freelance writer and a membership/development associate with a national Catholic reform organization.

Anna Zaros is from Huntersville, North Carolina, and now lives in Minneapolis, Minnesota, where she is planning a year of travel and volunteering abroad, including working as a teacher at Carmen Pampa University in Bolivia.

Acknowledgments

With one of us in academia and one of us working in writing and editing, both of us know that a book doesn't see publication without a lot of help along the way. We're honored to thank those who allowed us to see this project through to fruition.

We heartily thank Greg Pierce of ACTA Publications for believing in the voices of young adult Catholics. He came to us with the vision of a book about social justice written by young adult Catholics that would not be a collection of essays or sermons, but of personal stories. We thank him for this inspiration and for the opportunity to make it real, and for his generous encouragement and enthusiasm throughout the process.

Young Adult Catholics, the blog that first attracted Greg's attention, continues to be a space for Catholics in their twenties and thirties to share their passion for justice, their concerns for the future of God's people, and their stories of growing in faith. We thank the more than twenty writers who have shaped the blog over the years and who continue to contribute at youngadultcatholics-blog.com. We especially acknowledge Mike Sweitzer-Beckman for his leadership in the blog's formative stages.

Young Adult Catholics was started by members of CTA 20/30, a life-giving community of Catholics in their twenties and thirties on the quest for justice in the Church and in the world. Along with several of the book's writers, we are both members of CTA 20/30, and we thank this community for providing a spiritual home for those who hunger and thirst for justice.

Most of all, we thank the contributors to this book for their dedication to justice and their bravery in sharing their stories. Each of them has given generously of their time, authenticity, and vulnerability to make this vision a reality.

Finally, we thank you, our readers, for joining the conversation.

RELATED TITLES

The World as It Should Be:
Living Authentically in the Here and Now Kingdom of God

The Mass Is Never Ended:
Rediscovering Our Mission to Transform the World

Spirituality at Work:
10 Ways to Balance Your Life On-the-Job

Three books by publisher/writer Greg Pierce on how to work for justice in our daily lives on our jobs, with our loved ones, and in our community and civic involvements. 128-160 pages each, $10.95-$14.95

Catholic & College Bound
Catholic & Newly Married

Two helpful new books for young Catholics just starting out in life, listing five "challenges" and five "opportunities" for those in college or newly married. 64 pages each, $6.95

Grace Notes

Thirty-seven short story-essays by Brian Doyle, the editor of the University of Portland's award-winning magazine, that explore "the genius of American Catholicism" with insight, humor, passion, and joy. 160 pages, $14.95

Seeking the Truth of Things:
confessions of a (catholic) philosopher

An award-winning introduction to (catholic) philosophy by popular Loyola University of Chicago professor of business ethics Al Gini. 112 pages, $14.95

Flying in the Face of Tradition:
Listening to the Lived Experience of the Faithful

The controversial new book by Brother Louis DeThomasis, FSC, the former president of St. Mary's University of Minnesota, that explores the Catholic notion of "tradition" as a source of revelation as a way out of the current quandary in the Catholic Church. 102 pages, $12.95

Available from booksellers or call 800-397-2282
www.actapublications.com